THE BRISTOL BOYS

The untold story of Bristol's champion boxers

THE BRISTOL BOYS

The untold story of Bristol's champion boxers

Jack Allen

To all the Bristol Boys, past and present

First published in 2009 by Redcliffe Press Ltd.
81g Pembroke Road, Bristol BS8 3EA
T: 0117 973 7207
E: info@redcliffepress.co.uk
www.redcliffepress.co.uk

ISBN 978-1-906593-39-1

British Library Cataloguing-in-Publication Data
A catalogue record for this book is available from the British Library

Designed by Stephen Morris, smc@freeuk.com www.stephen-morris.co.uk

Printed by HSW, Tonypandy, Rhondda

The Hatchet Inn, Bristol, engraved by Trevor Haddrell: the best fighters of the day sparred in its ring. The Hatchet is still in business

Contents

The fight between Jack Randall and Martin The Baker gives an excellent idea of the scene of a prize fight towards the end of the great period of bare-knuckle boxing

INTRODUCTION

TODAY, VERY FEW BRISTOLIANS REALISE THEIR CITY CAN claim to be the birthplace of five world boxing champions who all held the title at various stages during a golden period of Bristol's sporting history. We're talking, of course, about bare-knuckle fighting and the heroes – Ben Brain, Jem Belcher, Henry Pearce, John Gully and Tom Cribb – were the very first sporting superstars. They were among the most famous celebrities in the land and held in the highest esteem by everyone from rogues and labourers up the highest echelons of society including royalty.

That they all came from Bristol or the surrounding area is quite astonishing but even more remarkable is the fact that they're almost unknown in the city today. Their names mean nothing to most Bristolians. No plaque, no statue. In fact the only public recognition that two of them ever existed can be seen in Panton Street, London – where the Tom Cribb public house displays a plaque on the wall stating the champion boxer once lived there – and at the Woolwich churchyard where his tomb can still be seen, and in the 'Gully Room' at the Rose and Crown pub in Wick in honour of John Gully who was born there in 1783.

The Hatchet Inn in Frogmore Street, Bristol dates back to 1606 and during the golden age of bare-knuckle fighting there was a boxing ring in its grounds where several of the great boxing champions of the day would turn up to spar or give exhibitions in the noble art of self-defence. A painting on a wall inside the pub relays this information.

But that's all there is. All there is to show for the great achievements of these fighting men. I hope this book will go some way to redress the omission and pay homage to five incredibly brave pugilists who brought huge fame and honour to the city.

From 1780 to 1820 boxing was the most popular spectator sport in England, even more popular than horse racing. It was not unusual for crowds of over forty thousand to attend one of the fights: quite remarkable when one considers the modes of transport and the appalling state of the roads at the time. The fans would arrive on foot, horseback, by cart and carriage and the excitement generated by a fight between the leading protagonists of the day was as intense as any sporting occasion in the modern era, whether boxing, football, cricket or rugby.

What obviously added to the thrill and excitement was the fact that boxing in those days was illegal and if caught the participants would be charged with 'unlawful assembly' or 'inciting a riot' and be bound over to keep the peace. Consequently fights were held at secret venues which were often changed on the day of the fight in order to make it more difficult for the magistrates to act.

Ironically the men behind the fights were city 'Swells', or 'The Fancy' as they were known, a group of monied and often aristocratic patron-gamblers. They were the financial backers of the pugilists and each had their own particular favourite. Both the Prince of Wales, later George IV, and the Duke of Clarence, later William IV, were active sponsors and turned up regularly to see the action.

The one place in London where 'The Fancy' liked to be seen was the Fives Court in Little St Martin's Lane. Here

The Fives Court, Little St Martin's Lane, London. Engraving by Charles Turner after a painting by T Blake

deals were done and challenges made and sometimes exhibition fights were fought. Lord Byron, an avid supporter, would often participate in sparring sessions at the Fives Court against other enthusiastic amateurs as a way of keeping fit, wearing gloves of course.

Professional fights were a different matter altogether. They were bloody and brutal affairs fought with 'the raw uns' (bare fists) with huge amounts of money being wagered on which pugilist would draw first blood, win each round or be the eventual winner. A boxing ring in those days was nothing like today's sophisticated, safety-conscious structure. It usually consisted of a hastily-built raised wooden platform surrounded by a wooden fence which boxers would sometimes use to their advantage by throwing their

RULES

TO BE OBSERVED IN ALL BATTLES ON THE STAGE

I. THAT a ſquare of a Yard be chalked in the middle of the Stage; and on every freſh ſet-to after a fall, or being parted from the rails, each Second is to bring his Man to the ſide of the ſquare, and place him oppoſite to the other, and till they are fairly ſet-to at the Lines, it ſhall not be lawful for one to ſtrike at the other.

II. That, in order to prevent any Diſputes, the time a Man lies after a fall, if the Second does not bring his Man to the ſide of the ſquare, within the ſpace of half a minute, he ſhall be deemed a beaten Man.

III. That in every main Battle, no perſon whatever ſhall be upon the Stage, except the Principals and their Seconds; the ſame rule to be obſerved in bye-battles, except that in the latter, Mr. Broughton is allowed to be upon the Stage to keep decorum, and to aſſiſt Gentlemen in getting to their places, provided always he does not interfere in the Battle; and whoever pretends to infringe theſe Rules to be turned immediately out of the houſe. Every body is to quit the Stage as ſoon as the Champions are ſtripped, before the ſet-to.

IV. That no Champion be deemed beaten, unleſs he fails coming up to the line in the limited time, or that his own Second declares him beaten. No Second is to be allowed to aſk his man's Adversary any queſtions, or adviſe him to give out.

V. That in bye-battles, the winning man to have two-thirds of the Money given, which ſhall be publicly divided upon the Stage, notwithſtanding any private agreements to the contrary.

VI. That to prevent Diſputes, in every main Battle the Principals ſhall, on coming on the Stage, chooſe from among the gentlemen preſent two Umpires, who ſhall abſolutely decide all Diſputes that may ariſe about the Battle; and if the two Umpires cannot agree, the ſaid Umpires to chooſe a third, who is to determine it.

VII. That no perſon is to hit his Adverſary when he is down, or ſeize him by the ham, the breeches, or any part below the waiſt: a man on his knees to be reckoned down.

Broughton's rules

Jack Broughton: champion of England for 16 years

opponent against it. Occasionally the platform might be done away with and the area covered in turf and a roped ring put in place.

The very first rules of boxing were drawn up by Jack Broughton from Cirencester – champion of England from 1734 to 1750 – after he'd delivered a fatal blow on an opponent in a bout in 1743. Broughton ran his own amphitheatre in the Tottenham Court Road and is regarded as the founding father of the modern art of self-defence. His rules stipulated that a round would end when one man went to ground as a result of being floored. His handlers then had thirty seconds to revive him and position him in his corner ready to come up to scratch (hence the expression) which was a line drawn across the centre of the ring.

There was no limit to the number of rounds. Fights could go on for over an hour and would end only when one of the participants failed to come up to scratch or signalled their retirement. Fighters weren't allowed to hit below the belt or strike a man when he was down. Some wrestling holds were allowed but only above the waist.

To prevent disputes each fighter had an umpire to act on his behalf and if the two couldn't agree they went to a third, neutral, umpire. Pugilists were incredibly brave men and during the course of a bare-knuckle fight it was not unusual for heads to become so battered and swollen that their features were barely recognisable. Sometimes the seconds, fearing for their fighter's life, would end the contest by throwing in the towel.

It was not until 1869 that the eighth Marquis of Queensberry introduced the Queensberry rules which insisted on the use of padded gloves, three-minute rounds and strict supervision of the type of blows permitted and a designated target area.

Such was the life of a professional boxer in those far-off days. The brutality and bloodshed of bare-knuckle fighting is something that in our more civilised times most people find distasteful but in the late 1700s and early 1800s boxing was incredibly popular and a significant element of English life. It is thus an important part not only of our sporting but also our social history. We shouldn't let our squeamishness detract from the great achievements of the Bristol Boys and perhaps it is time they were officially recognised by a statue or plaque in a public place as a reminder of their courage and the glory they brought to the city.

JACK SLACK

NO MENTION OF BEN BRAIN, JEM BELCHER, HENRY PEARCE, John Gully and Tom Cribb would be complete without first some reference being made to Jack Slack. Although, after becoming champion in 1750, he was known as 'Jack Slack of Bristol' he was actually born at Thorpe near Norwich in 1721. As a youngster Slack showed the skills and bravery that were later to make him famous in the boxing rings around the country and when the travelling fairs were in the Norwich area he set up his own boxing booth and took on all comers. He soon made enough money to open up a butchery business with his brother.

It wasn't long before Jack Slack became recognised as the champion of Norfolk and on 24 June 1744 he defeated Daniel Smith, the Suffolk champion. Smith, however, wasn't satisfied with the outcome and issued a challenge in a contemporary journal. It provides a good example of the way boxers and their patrons conducted pugilistic affairs at that time. It was the practice to issue a public challenge as it generated interest in the fight and was in effect free advertising.

> I, Daniel Smith, the Suffolk champion do once more invite Mr Jack Slack, the Norfolk champion, to meet and fight me for the sum of forty guineas, and, though I had the misfortune to be defeated by him before, am sure I am much superior in the art of boxing, and doubt not but I shall give him and the company entire satisfaction.
>
> DANIEL SMITH

Jack Slack: an unpopular champion

The Norfolk butcher replied:

> I, John Slack, the Norfolk champion, do accept the challenge, and will be certain to meet and fight the above hero for the said sum, at the time and place above mentioned; and don't doubt but I shall support the character I have hitherto maintained.
>
> JOHN SLACK

The two men fought a terrific return-battle near Framlingham Castle, Suffolk in front of thousands of people and once again Slack emerged victorious. Now confident that he could make a name for himself amongst the London boxers Slack sold his share in the butcher's business and travelled to the capital in 1748. The champion at the time was the great Jack Broughton, the man who'd formulated the very first rules of boxing and who ran an academy for boxing in the Tottenham Court Road teaching the art of self defence to city swells.

To get himself noticed Slack thought it would be a good idea to challenge Broughton's finest pupil, a man called Ned Hunt, for a sum of 50 guineas. Poor Hunt accepted but was so badly beaten he never fought again and Broughton, being the kind-hearted gentleman he was, put Hunt in charge of his famous amphitheatre where he gave boxing lessons to, amongst others, the Prince of Wales. Slack returned to Norwich in triumph and the following year, 1749, made a trip to Bristol, the town where his wife's mother was born. It was during this visit he made the decision to set up a school for boxing at the Guildhall Tavern, little realising at the time the influential role it was later to play in the history of British boxing.

In January 1750 Slack tasted defeat for the very first time. For some unknown reason he'd picked a quarrel with the former champion George Taylor which resulted in their being matched in the ring. Taylor was well into his forties and hadn't fought for years and was taking a bit of a battering when Slack, rushing in to finish the job, tripped and fell heavily and was unable to beat the newly introduced rule of coming up to scratch within the allotted 30 seconds.

Slack was an angry and bitter man at having been beaten

Jack Slack in fighting pose

George Taylor: the first man to beat Jack Slack

in that unfamiliar fashion. The person he blamed for his defeat was the man who had introduced the rule, the champion Jack Broughton himself. Months later the two bumped into each other at Hounslow Races and a furious row developed. Broughton grabbed a riding whip and struck Slack across the legs whereupon Slack picked up a carving knife and made for the champion. Both men had to be restrained. The only way they could settle their differences would be for them to meet in the ring.

The fight took place at Broughton's Amphitheatre on 11 April 1750. It attracted enormous interest amongst 'The Fancy' and people travelled from miles around to queue for hours at the doors. It was a massive occasion in London's sporting calendar and the Prince of Wales and members of his family sat in a purpose-built box to watch the event. Huge bets were laid on the outcome of the fight, and it was estimated over a million pounds was gambled on the result. Broughton's patron, the Duke of Cumberland – the notorious 'Butcher of Culloden' – had backed his man heavily to win the fight and stood to lose £10,000 if the hitherto undefeated Broughton was beaten.

Slack wasn't a big man by today's standards. He stood just 5' 8½" tall and weighed nearly 14 stone. Compact would be the polite way to describe him. Broughton, on the other hand was the exact opposite, standing 6' tall and weighing nearly the same, he resembled a sculptured Roman gladiator with the grace and finesse of an athlete. The fight lasted only 14 minutes and ended when Slack landed one of his famous 'chopper' blows right between the champion's eyes. The effect was terrible. The eyes puffed up and blood trickled out from beneath the eyelids. Broughton was blinded and the 'Butcher of Culloden' yelled in anger, 'What are you doing Broughton? You can't fight! We shall lose our money!' Broughton replied, 'I can't see my man your Highness! I'm blind but not beat! Place me before my man so I may see him, and I'll gain the day yet!' Slack continued to hit him again and again until at last the mighty Broughton cried out, 'I'm done! By God, I'm done!' and Slack was declared the winner.

Jack Slack wasn't a popular champion. He had none of the class and poise that Broughton had brought to the ring and he didn't conduct himself in the same gentlemanly

Jack Broughton: 'a sculptured Roman gladiator'

manner as the previous champion had done. On the contrary he often abused all the rules Broughton had drawn up and resorted to a 'no-holds-barred' style of fighting. He held on to the title for ten years during which time he toured the country with his travelling booth giving exhibitions and taking on and defeating all comers. Two such incidents are worth recounting.

On one occasion he fought the strong man from a travelling circus, a Frenchman called Mons. Petit for £100 a-side. The battle took place at Harleston, a little village south of Norwich on Thursday, 29 July 1751. Petit may have been his name but by all accounts he was anything but small. Standing 6' 4" and weighing over 16 stones Petit started the fight by grabbing Slack by the throat in an attempt to strangle him, then throwing him over the rails. It soon developed into a no-holds-barred fight and Slack was taking a beating. After the first few rounds the betting was a guinea to a shilling on the Frenchman. Slack, however, composed himself and as Petit began to tire he started peppering his face with powerful punches which resulted in one of his eyes becoming closed. After 25 minutes Slack was on top and he managed to throw the 'man mountain' out of the ring whereupon the Frenchman disgracefully walked away. The fight followers called this 'rogueing it' as it was generally thought Petit had quit whilst still strong enough to continue.

Another story worth recounting happened four years later when Slack was touring the West Country and was challenged by a Kingswood miner named Cornelius Harris, a brute with a notorious reputation. There wasn't a man in the area prepared to fight 'King Cole' Harris, a nickname derived from the grime and coal dust that permanently covered his skin. One story relates to the time Harris and his girlfriend went for a Sunday afternoon stroll and Harris came back alone. A search for the missing girl found her dead beside the body of a former lover. Harris was the obvious suspect but in the days before the Public Prosecutor

Mons. Petit: walked away from a fight

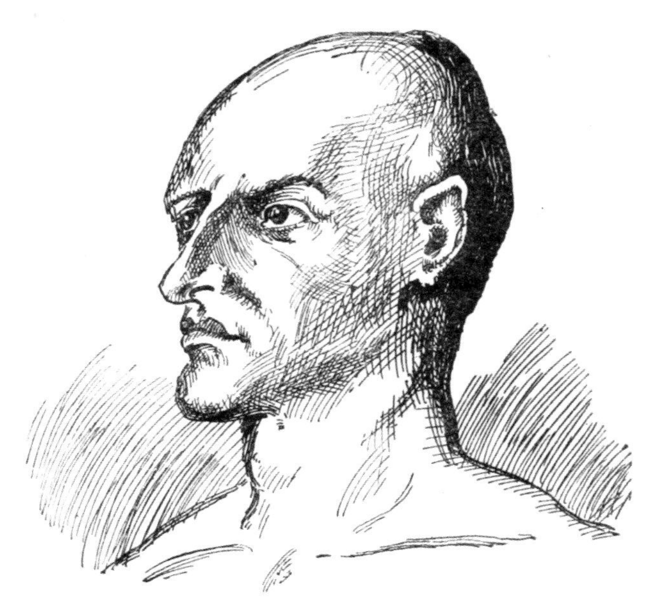

Bill 'The Nailer' Stevens: ended Jack Slack's reign as champion

nobody had the courage to accuse him of the crime. This murderous, probably insane, thug had many battles on the village green, all of which he won. Anyone stupid enough to quarrel with him was invited down the pit to settle their differences, often never to return.

When Jack Slack brought his travelling booth to Bristol 'King Cole' Harris sent out the message he wanted to challenge him for the championship. In those days a champion had no option but to accept a challenge or else he had to forfeit the title. Slack accepted but on learning the history of the man made it a condition they fight for 100 guineas a-side. He was hoping the sum would prove to be too much for Harris and the fight would have to be called off. To his dismay Harris found the money, probably through extortion, and the fight was arranged to take place at Kingswood, near Bristol on 13 March 1755. It was a brutal contest with both fighters hammering away at each other with blows that would kill most normal men. They'd fought to the point of complete exhaustion when Slack summoned up his remaining ounces of strength and delivered a crushing blow on Harris's head. The fight was over. Slack took his winnings and beat a hasty retreat before the wild man of Kingswood recovered.

After another five years of life on the road Slack was matched at 100 guineas a-side by the Duke of Cumberland to defend his title against Bill 'The Nailer' Stevens from Birmingham who was under the patronage of the Duke of York. The pair met on 17 June 1760 at the Tennis Court in James Street and Slack – now no longer in the prime of life – was finally defeated. There was a tremendous roar from the boxing fans present when they realised that Jack Slack's reign as champion of England had at last come to an end.

On losing his title Slack returned to his former trade as a butcher and opened up a shop in Chandos Street, London, dividing his time between business and teaching the art of self-defence. Although he was never a skilful fighter, the tag 'ex-Champion' ensured Slack had a regular clientele. One such apprentice, George Meggs, had travelled up from Bristol to try and make a name for himself amongst the London bruisers. After testing him out in private and deciding Meggs was good enough, Slack put up £200 of his own money and issued a challenge to Bill Stevens which the champion readily accepted. The fight was on but then Slack began to have second thoughts about the quality of his protégé. He resorted to bribing 'The Nailer' to lose the fight which Stevens duly did, and in such corrupt and disgraceful circumstances Meggs became the champion.

Once the part he'd played in fixing the fight became widely known Slack's reputation in boxing circles lay in ruins. However, he stuck to his business as a butcher and seemed to prosper until his death in 1778. Slack's name would have faded away completely had not a rapid succession of champion boxers begin to emerge from the Bristol school he'd established earlier in his career. Amongst them was his very own grandson, the great Jem Belcher, who grew up to be perhaps the most skilful boxer who ever lived and certainly the first sporting icon of the modern age. Add to that the names of Ben Brain, Henry Pearce, John Gully and Tom Cribb and you get some idea of the importance of the role play by Jack Slack in the careers of the Bristol Boys.

'BIG' BEN BRAIN

Ben Brain was born in Kingswood in 1753 and although he became known as 'Big' Ben Brain his actual size didn't do justice to the nickname. He was only 5' 10" tall and weighed just over 13 stone which by today's standards of super-heavyweight boxers and indeed even amongst his contemporaries made him rather small. Despite all that he was a valiant fighter and had a career that spanned 20 years.

As soon as he reached the age of 12 Brain began work as a miner at the Kingswood Colliery where amongst the tough, unruly men he worked alongside he soon established a reputation as being good with the 'raw uns'. By the time he was 20 Brain had defeated all local opposition including Bob Harris, 'The Cock of Kingswood', and even Jack Clayton the Shropshire Champion. As there was no one left good enough to take him on he was forced to travel to London to further his career. His mentor at that time was the great Jack Slack, the conqueror of Broughton and former champion, who'd settled in Bristol many years previously to work as a butcher and establish a school for boxing at the Guildhall Tavern.

Slack for reasons already explained wasn't a popular man in the Capital. Brain, a shy and retiring man, didn't push himself and had to wait years before he got a fight. In the meantime however, he'd taken a job as a coal porter at a wharf near The Strand and distinguished himself amongst his fellow labourers as a man who could handle himself.

Ben Brain: shy and retiring

Brain had been living and working in London for 12 years and must have been 33-years-old when he had his first recorded fight in the capital. There were probably numerous fights in the interim period, low key affairs held at travelling fairs or private rooms in pubs or sporting clubs. On 31 October 1786 his principal backer, the Duke of Hamilton, finally matched him against John Boone, 'The Fighting Grenadier', at a spot called Long Fields – now the site of the British Museum. Boone had a reputation as a fierce hitter and his blows were said to be like the kick from a horse. As early as the second round he landed a crunching blow between Brain's eyes which caused them to swell so much that he couldn't see. The incident caused so much excitement that the crowd rushed the ring, causing it to collapse, but during the time it took to repair it and restore order a surgeon present at the fight whipped out a lancet and bled Brain so that he was able to continue. Brain took advantage of this bit of luck and after a long and brutal fight lasting 40 minutes he emerged the winner but didn't box again for another two years.

Brain's next fight, again arranged for him by the Duke of Hamilton, was against an Irishman called William Corbally. The two men met on 31 December 1788 at Navestock in Essex. It was a bitterly cold day and snow lay on the ground all around the ring but 'Big' Ben managed to come out the winner after 20 minutes of fierce fighting. This victory over Corbally put Brain in line for a title fight against the unbeaten champion, the great Tom Johnson. A fight was arranged at £500 aside but unfortunately Brain had to forfeit his £100 deposit when he became ill.

When eventually fit enough to fight again he was matched against Jack Jacombs, the Birmingham champion, at Banbury on 23 October 1789. The fight didn't start too well for 'Big' Ben. Jacombs fought with a style that was considered unmanly by many of 'The Fancy'. He relied on driving and bruising his opponent into the railings rather than fair and open fighting with the fists. Jacombs's ferocity took Ben by surprise and he had to keep dodging around to avoid the blows and then falling to end the round. These tactics annoyed his opponent's supporters and they soon began to let their feelings be known. The mood got quite ugly until Brain finally stood up to Jacombs and landed a

Tom Tring, the Big Porter of Carlton House

tremendous blow which changed the course of the fight. After a hard-fought battle that lasted 36 rounds and for one hour and 26 minutes Jacombs finally surrendered.

'Big' Ben's next fight was against the giant Tom Tring, a protégé of the Prince of Wales, the future George IV. Tring's is an interesting story for he started life as a sedan chairman working at Carlton House, the Prince's official residence which stood at the corner of St James's Park in London. He was by all accounts a magnificent physical specimen standing 6' 2½" tall and perfectly proportioned. The artist Sir Joshua Reynolds used 'the finest made man in the country' as a model on many occasions and he became so popular that the Prince promoted him to the job of porter. He stood at the main entrance at Carlton House to be admired by visitors. It wasn't long before certain members of 'The Fancy', saw an opportunity to make some money and encouraged by the Prince, a great fan of boxing, Tring was put under the tutorage of the champion Tom Johnson to learn the art of defence and attack. Tring had three fights which he won quite convincingly and the Prince then backed him for £1000 against any man in the country except, of course, Tom Johnson.

Ben Brain took up the challenge and the two men met for a paltry ten guineas a-side at Dartford on 18 December 1789. The Prince watched the fight covered in furs from the box seat of his drag which was positioned close to the ring. Contemporary accounts describe the Prince in those days as:

> A heartless dandy, and unprincipled egotist miscalled 'the first gentleman of Europe', without a particle of the gentleman in his whole composition.

Bristolian Bill Hooper, 'The Tinman'

It was a good description, for when Brain beat Tring quite easily after only 12 rounds that lasted just 19 minutes the Prince displayed his heartless nature by dismissing Tom Tring from his service.

Brain's next fight was against Bill Hooper, another Bristolian and known as 'The Tinman' because of his trade. Hooper roamed the countryside from village to village leading a gypsy life-style selling pots and pans and getting into numerous scrapes along the way. He soon acquired a reputation of being handy with his fists and his prowess came to the attention of Lord Barrymore, one of the leading lights of 'The Fancy'. Under his patronage The Tinman kept winning and made the unpopular Barrymore very rich and in effect became his minder. Eventually he was matched against Ben Brain and the fight came off on 30 August 1790 near Newbury in Berkshire. The fight itself was a farce with Hooper having no intention of mixing it with his fellow townsman. The contest went on for three and a half hours and 180 rounds and was eventually called a draw. Rumour had it that Hooper was boxing to Barrymore's instructions and was what they called in those days 'fighting for darkness' when all bets would be declared null and void. However nothing was ever proved.

Ben Brain was now the leading contender for the title and his previous two fights were in effect just warm-up bouts before the match against the champion Tom Johnson could be arranged. The show-down attracted enormous public interest and over £100,000 in bets were laid with Johnson the 7-4 on favourite. The two men finally met on 17 January 1791 at Wratham in Kent, a small village on the

Tom Johnson: ceded the championship to Ben Brain after a terrific knockdown blow

main road between Maidstone and London. The thousands of spectators who gathered on the hill overlooking the arena cheered the pugilists as they entered the ring and all the 'Swell' sportsmen of the day, including the Prince of Wales, were full of admiration at the fine condition both men had got themselves into. An uncanny silence fell over the crowd as they faced each other in the centre of the ring.

There was a sensational beginning to the fight. In the first few minutes 'Big' Ben landed one of the powerful right-hand punches he was famous for and split Johnson's nose wide open. The champion landed flat on his face and it looked for all the world as if the fight was over before it had even begun. Somehow or other Johnson's men managed to get their fighter to come up to scratch before the allotted 30 seconds and the fight continued with a ferocity that even in those bare-knuckle days was very hard to stomach. Both men went at it hammer-and-tongs in one of the most brutal fights ever recorded. During the course of the contest Johnson landed a blow on Brain's forehead that broke two of the fingers on his right hand, rendering it practically useless. Round after round Brain knocked Johnson to the ground and the champion got weaker and weaker but still he came back for more. He was taking such a terrible battering and his face became so horrible to look at that spectators close to the action shuddered at the sight. Lord Byron, who was one who witnessed the fight, later wrote in his journal, 'That it was almost impossible to distinguish Johnson's face from the hind part of the head.'

The fight had lasted 18 rounds and for only 31 minutes when Johnson received a terrific knockdown blow that left him senseless and bleeding. Not wishing their man to suffer any further damage his seconds threw in the towel and 'Big' Ben Brain from Kingswood became champion of England which in those days of course meant the world. It was the great Tom Johnson's final fight. He never challenged for the title again. After the fight the *Daily Advertiser* reported,

> Though Johnson was so heavily punished, in appearance Ben seemed little hurt, and on the Monday following he displayed great agility in a sparring match at the Grecian Theatre, in The Strand.

Three years were to elapse before 'Big' Ben Brain was called upon to defend his title against the number one challenger

Will Wood, known as 'The Coachman'. The fight was scheduled to take place on 24 February 1794 and although Ben Brain hadn't been in the best of health in the months leading up to the fight he was still reckoned to be the favourite. However, just before the contest Ben was taken very ill and the fight had to be cancelled. His condition deteriorated rapidly after that and he died on 8 April 1794 of a liver disease at his home on the Grays Inn Road. He was just 41-years-old and was buried in St Sepulchre's Church in Skinner Street, Snow Hill where the inscription on his tomb, written by a fellow boxer read:

> Farewell, ye honours of my brow!
> Victorious wreaths farewell!
> One blow from Death has laid me low
> By whom such brave ones fell
> Yet bravely I'll dispute this prize
> Nor yield, though out of breath
> 'Tis not a fall – I yet shall rise
> And conquer even death!

Ben Brain was the first of the great Bristol heroes, a man described by Pierce Egan, the most famous boxing writer of his day, as one who 'Always appeared clean and respectable, mild and sociable.' It is worth noting that the Bristol Boys were far from arrogant bullies. They were all very modest, honest and decent souls who – endowed with great courage, skill and stamina – rose to the very top of their hard profession and put the name of Bristol firmly on the sporting map. The cry of 'He's a Bristol man!' was beginning to be heard at boxing rings around the country.

JEM BELCHER
'NAPOLEON OF THE RING'

BORN ON 15 APRIL 1781 IN AN OLD DOUBLE-GABLED HOUSE that stood in the grounds of St James's churchyard in Bristol, Jem Belcher was the grandson of the famous pugilist Jack Slack who'd opened up a school for boxing in the city many years previously. Fighting was in the Belcher blood. His brother Tom was a respected boxer and there are reports that one of his sisters once fought a battle with another woman that lasted fifty minutes.

Jem's first contest of note was as a 12-year-old lad at the St James's Fair that was held annually in the churchyard his house overlooked. He was matched against a colliery boy from Kingswood and his brother-in-law Bob Watson, himself a pugilist, was quoted at the time as saying Jem was, 'one of those lissom, wiry, "varminty" lads who didn't know what fear was.' Jem won the fight and gave an impressive display of the speed and skill that would soon be turning him into a fighting phenomenon and one of the major sporting celebrities of the late eighteenth and early nineteenth centuries.

Bristol at that time had the reputation of being the worst governed municipality in the kingdom. The watchmen whose job it was to protect life and property were themselves drunkards in league with criminals and prostitutes. The entertainment of the day was bull baiting, bear baiting, cock fighting and prize fighting, the latter being by far the most popular. Bristolians apparently loved fighting and all domestic disputes and questions of rivalry in either trade or love were usually settled by the fist.

Jem Belcher: 'Napoleon of the ring'

Young Belcher grew up in this climate of lawlessness and started working life with Bob Watson as a butcher's boy delivering the meat around the city riding on a pony. He

St James's Fair, Bristol as depicted by Samuel Colman. *Courtesy Bristol Museums Galleries and Archives*

had his first professional fight at the age of 16 at the Lansdown Fair near Bath, where his opponent, a local youth named Sam Lowatt, was being given such a beating the fight was stopped very early on by a well-known pugilist of the day named Bob Britton. Britton was courting Lowatt's sister and thought it wouldn't be appropriate to let the fight continue. Immediately an angry Jem challenged Britton to fight instead and a match was arranged for a purse ten guineas a-side to be held on 6 March 1798 at Hanham, then a village near Bristol. A crowd of nearly 2000 people turned up to see it and Britton, because of the enormous difference in size, age and experience, started as the two-to-one favourite.

Britton began the fight as if to annihilate Jem but the youngster ducked and dived and began to lead him such a merry dance that the older man got out of breath and began to lose his temper. Jem easily avoided Britton's mad rushes and began to strike back at lightning speed until Britton's face resembled a jelly and he was nearly blind through the swelling around his eyes. Jem had his opponent at his mercy and was giving him such a fearful beating that after 33 minutes the fight was stopped when Britton failed to come up to the mark.

This fight established Jem's reputation in Bristol. He became something of a hero and life as a butcher's boy came to a premature stop. His family, realising they had another potential champion in their midst, made a collection and Jem was sent to London to further his boxing

Jem Belcher, from a painting by John Berridge

career. A friend of his father made sure that Jem was introduced to the rich and powerful who controlled the sport.

'The Fancy' first arranged for Jem to box an exhibition in private so they could gauge for themselves just how good he was. The former champion he was sparring against was hopelessly outclassed and had no answer to the speed and skill of 'The Bristol Youth' as Jem was now being called. As a result of the trial Jem was immediately matched against the hitherto unbeaten Tom 'Paddington' Jones. Jem's handlers, Mr Fletcher Reid and John Cullingham, had tried desperately to keep the result of the trial a secret so that they could get better odds on their man but the word had got out and Jem started as the 6-4 on favourite.

The fight against Jones took place, three days before Jem's nineteenth birthday on 12 April 1799, close to Wormwood Scrubs and after sixteen rounds lasting 33 minutes Jem was declared the winner. Victory turned him into an overnight sensation. With his handsome looks and impeccable manners he became the most elegant and widely respected prize fighter of the period. He started to acquire all manner of nicknames including 'The New Bristol Wonder' and the 'The Napoleon Of The Ring' because of his remarkable likeness to the little French General. None of the establishment swells who followed boxing had ever seen a man as quick as Belcher. Such was the speed of his punch that spectators could see the results of the blows as they landed but could not see them being delivered.

Tom 'Paddington' Jones: unbeaten until he met the young Belcher

Jack Bartholomew: held Jem Belcher to a draw

As a result of Jem's new-found fame in the capital no one really wanted to fight him until finally a man called Jack Bartholomew threw his hat into the ring. The match took place on 15 August 1799 at George's Row on the Uxbridge Road. Belcher hadn't trained properly for the fight because he'd seriously underestimated his opponent and was surprisingly held to a draw after 51 rounds that lasted 40 minutes.

Of course neither party was satisfied with the result and a rematch took place on Finchley Common on 15 May 1800 for a purse of 300 guineas. Again it was a really close-fought, savage affair with both men at various stages in the fight looking as though he'd won it. However in the seventeenth round Belcher put the result beyond dispute when he caught Bartholomew with a terrific body blow from which he never recovered. Even though the fight had lasted barely 20 minutes some claimed it was one of the most brutal battles they'd ever seen.

Immediately after this victory Belcher issued a challenge to Daniel Mendoza to fight for the championship which had become vacant because John Jackson the previous holder had retired from boxing. Mendoza accepted Jem's challenge but the magistrates had got wind of the fight and Mendoza was arrested and bailed. The contest had to be called off for if Mendoza broke his bail conditions he'd forfeit a large sum of money.

By now Belcher had amassed a considerable fortune and acquired legions of fans so the search was on to find a new

Daniel Mendoza: arrested by the magistrates

Andrew Gamble: lost to Belcher in nine minutes

opponent. Jem Belcher was now 'box office' and 'The Fancy' wanted to cash in. Eventually a stone mason by the name of Andrew Gamble, the Irish champion and a man who came with a formidable reputation, stepped forward to take up the challenge. Excitement ran high amongst 'The Fancy' and huge amounts of money were riding on the result of the fight but just four days before the bout Belcher was attacked by four men in Chelsea, no doubt in an attempt to scupper the fight. Fortunately, Belcher managed to beat off his attackers and escape unhurt and the fight went ahead, in front of an enormous crowd on Wimbledon Common on 22 December, 1800. The odds were 6-4 in favour of Belcher even though at 5' 11" and just 12 stone he was much the smaller man.

A contemporary report gave a round-by-round summary of the fight:

> ROUND 1. After some sparring, Gamble made play, but was prettily parried by Belcher, who, with unequalled celebrity, planted in return three severe facers; they soon closed, and Belcher being aware of his opponent's strength, dropped.
> ROUND 2. Belcher full of spirit advanced towards Gamble who retreated. Jem made a feint with his right hand, and with his left struck Gamble so severely over the right eye, as not only to close it immediately, but knock him down with uncommon violence.
> ROUND 4. Belcher, full of coolness and self-possession, showed first rate science. His blows were well directed, and severe, particularly one in the neck, which brought Gamble down. (Odds 10-1 Belcher was the winner)

The fight lasted only another round. It was all over in just nine minutes. Gamble had no answer to the speed and skill of the 'Bristol Youth' and failed to answer to the call of 'Time' at the beginning of the round six. Pigeons carried the news of Belcher's victory back to his native city and the church bells of Bristol rang out in celebration. Victory gave Belcher the Championship he always seemed destined to hold and now there was no shortage of opponents prepared to challenge him for the title. One such fighter was Joe Berks, a man who trained on raw eggs to improve his wind and raw meat to make him savage. He picked a quarrel with Belcher on Wimbledon Common whilst Jem was watching another fight. The two had an impromptu set-to in the ring which lasted 19 minutes and although Berks was soundly beaten many who saw it reckoned if they fought again Berks would be in with a chance.

A rematch was arranged on 25 November 1801 at Hurley Bottom, near Maidenhead. It was a nasty and brutal affair as a contemporary account informs us:

> **ROUND 1**. Several severe blows were exchanged. Berks showed in better style than usual. He put in a well directed hit under his antagonist's right eye, who staggered. The men closed and both fell.
> **ROUND 5**. Belcher made a feint with his left hand, and with his right put in so sharp a hit on the nose of his opponent that he laid it open, and brought him down with great violence.
> **ROUND 6**. Much shy fighting, Berks keeping out of distance. Belcher at length struck Berks over the forehead, and cut him again severely; the blood now issued so freely from his wounds, that Lee (his second) could scarcely find handkerchiefs sufficient to keep him clean.

The fight ended in the sixteenth round when Berks's seconds intervened to stop their man from taking further punishment. He was exhausted and his face was in a dreadful state whereas Belcher in comparison was unmarked. As soon as the fight was over Belcher once again challenged Daniel Mendoza but again the former champion declined. After their battle both Berks and Belcher were arrested for disturbing the peace but whereas Belcher was able to put up bail Berks was deserted by his backers and spent three months in Reading Gaol.

Joe Berks: three months in Reading Gaol

A feud developed between the two men and after another skirmish between them at Camberwell Fair they decided to fight again the following day for a purse of 30 guineas. Once again Belcher gave Berks a terrible beating and cut him so badly that it was impossible to distinguish his features. Belcher again emerged unscathed.

The magistrates started hounding Belcher and it was becoming increasingly more difficult for him to get fights so his next contest against Jack Firby, 'The Young Ruffian', had to be carefully planned and the venue kept secret. It took place on 12 April 1803 just outside the village of Linton, 15 miles from Newmarket. Because of the secrecy surrounding the fight not even the locals knew it was taking

Belcher versus Andrew Gamble, the Irish champion. © *Getty Images*

place so when they saw crowds of people streaming through their village at six o'clock in the morning they thought they were being chased by the French! A purse of 100 guineas was subscribed by 'The Fancy' and the two men agreed to split it 90-10 to the winner.

ROUND 4. Both combatants rallied and both put in some severe blows. They closed, Belcher fell, and while on his knees Firby struck him. A cry of 'Foul! Foul!' resounded from all sides. Belcher appealed for a decision of the point, but wished to go on rather than take advantage of such circumstances. At this point a parson and a constable arrived from Linton, and endeavoured to prevent the further progress of the battle; but the combatants, not paying much attention to the sacred cloth or the legal staff, continued.
ROUND 9. At the first onset Belcher put in a severe blow over his antagonist's right eye and immediately resuming a defensive attitude very cheerfully said, 'How do you like that Johnny?' Firby made a

desperate blow but over-reached himself and fell; Belcher smiled and while he was down pointed at him with great irony.

It was a one-sided fight which Belcher never looked like losing. The contest altogether had lasted 20 minutes when finally Firby was persuaded to quit by his friends. It was another easy win for Jem who again finished the fight unmarked.

Belcher was now 22-years-old and at the very pinnacle of his fame. A nineteenth-century fashion and sporting icon, he had wealth and good looks and mixed in the highest echelons of society, but then, on 24 July 1803, an incident took place which wrecked his boxing career. Whilst playing rackets with a friend he was struck in the eye by the ball. The surgeon tried in vain to save the eye but it had to be removed and Belcher was forced to retire from the ring. He became a publican at The Two Brewers in Wardour Street and stayed there for the next two years, getting badly out of condition. He kept in touch with boxing, and invited a boxer friend of his from Bristol – Henry Pearce – to come to London and try for the title. Pearce, also known as 'The Game Chicken', did much more than that: he went on to beat some of the men Belcher had beaten and claimed the Championship itself.

Rather than rejoice that his protégé was now champion, Belcher became bitter and, despite being blind in one eye, challenged Pearce for the title. The Chicken didn't want to fight his former friend but as champion he could not decline. See the following chapter for details.

Belcher was fighting a lost cause and the longer the fight went on the greater became his disadvantage. After 18 desperate rounds that lasted 35 minutes Belcher raised his hand and murmured 'Hen Pearce, I can't fight thee no more.'

Henry Pearce: 'The Game Chicken'

After the fight Belcher returned once again to the life of a publican but still he wasn't finished. He desperately yearned for former glories and the trappings of success and on hearing the news that Henry Pearce had retired from boxing because of failing health Belcher declared that whoever stepped forward to claim the championship would have to fight him first. To everyone's surprise the man who took up the challenge was Tom Cribb whose patron, the celebrated Captain Barclay, put up 200 guineas a-side.

Cribb at this stage of his career was not considered good enough to contend for the title but Captain Barclay thought otherwise. Belcher was asked before he accepted the challenge if he was ready to fight again. His reply was typical. 'They think,' he said, 'because I have lost an eye anyone can beat me. If I had two eyes I could lick Cribb with one hand. Will I fight him? Yes of course I will. I'll let them see that I'm Jem Belcher yet!'

Cribb went off to Bromley in Kent to train with Captain Barclay whilst Belcher returned to his home city of Bristol to train on Clifton Downs with his brother-in-law Bob Watson. The fight took place on Tuesday, 8 April 1807 at Moulsey Hurst. The re-appearance of Belcher in a boxing ring created great excitement and guaranteed an enormous crowd which included the Duke of Clarence, later William IV. Belcher started the 6-4 favourite, even though Cribb was more than two stone heavier.

> **ROUND 5**. Belcher with his right hand put in a dreadful blow on Cribb's left eye, and in closing hit his opponent twice in the body, and threw him. (Odds 5-2 on Belcher.)
>
> **ROUND 6**. Cribb began to show symptoms of weakness. Belcher put in a hit, warding off which caused Cribb to fall.
>
> **ROUND 10**. Belcher commenced this round with great spirit, and gave Cribb some severe blows, without letting him have a chance; following and rallying his opponent to the ropes, when Cribb appearing quite fatigued fell. (The odds now rose 4-1 on Jem.)
>
> **ROUND 16**. The knowing ones were at this period of the battle, rather at a standstill with regard to sporting their money. Cribb, it was certain, by his appearance, had received severe punishment, but not enough to satisfy anything like his gluttony and Belcher's stamina had been considered on the decline previous to the contest, and it was apprehended that he could not last.

Tom Cribb: challenged and beat Belcher for the title

The eighteenth round proved to be the turning point of the fight. Belcher hit Cribb on the side of the head with such force that Cribb went down like a lump of lead and everyone thought the fight was over. Indeed the odds were five to one on Belcher. The crowd rushed the ring and in the confusion that followed Cribb was allowed more than the statutory thirty seconds to recover his senses and the fight was allowed to continue. In striking Cribb Belcher had badly damaged his right hand and wasn't able to use it properly after that. The fact that he managed to carry on for another twenty three rounds speaks volumes for his skill and courage but by the forty-first round he was finished. Cribb landed two vicious blows which sent Belcher crashing to the ropes where he fell utterly exhausted. It was the end of a sensational fight and Tom Cribb had taken a giant step in enhancing his own career.

By 1809 both Henry Pearce the 'Game Chicken' and John Gully had retired as champions and Tom Cribb, having gone on to beat Andrew Gamble, the Irish Champion, had now succeeded to the title. Jem Belcher, who had seconded Gamble in his fight with Cribb and lost a lot of money betting on the wrong result, was itching to get back in the ring with Cribb because of the way he felt he'd been robbed the first time they'd met. He firmly believed he could reclaim the championship and against all the advice of his friends and backers he challenged Cribb for the championship for a purse of 200 guineas.

The two men fought their return battle on 1 February 1809 on Epsom Downs, and again the fans turned up in their thousands. The name 'Belcher' still had a magic ring to it and for miles around all roads leading to the race course were jammed with vehicles of all descriptions. When the fighters appeared in the ring Cribb looked the picture of health. Standing 5' 10½" tall and weighing over 14 stone he was in much the better shape. Belcher in contrast, had sadly neglected himself over the past few years and looked anything but a fighter. He stood 5' 11½" tall and weighed in at 11 stone, 10 pounds.

Jem Belcher: skilful and courageous against Cribb

Despite his poor physical condition and the loss of an eye, Belcher did more than enough in the early rounds to show he'd lost none of his skill and courage. He rekindled memories of his glory days by giving Cribb an early boxing lesson and the crowd roared their appreciation. They sensed an upset.

In Memory of
JAMES BELCHER,
Late of St. Anne's Parish, Soho,
who died
The 30th of July, 1811,
AGED 30,
Universally regretted by all who knew him.

With patience to the last he did submit,
And murmur'd not at what the Lord thought fit,
HE with a Christian courage did resign
His soul to God at his appointed time!

The inscription on Belcher's tomb at Marylebone burial ground

ROUND 5. Belcher put in right and left hits; but it was once more evident that he'd lamed his right hand. Cribb again rallied successfully, and threw his opponent.

ROUND 6. Belcher now, in order to avoid his adversary's superior strength, hit out, and successfully planted a blow at arms length with his lame hand on the spot he had before severely struck under the ear, and which was also the precise place in which Gregson put in his tremendous blow in their last contest. The blood issued with great force; they closed and Belcher threw Cribb a cross buttock. Cribb's gluttony, however was well known, odds were even now 4-1 in his favour.

ROUND 11. Cribb forced the fighting, as in the preceding round, and again threw Belcher. Both Belcher's hands were now injured, and Cribb kept the lead he had gained.

31st and FINAL ROUND. It was piteous to see this once renowned and brave champion contending against nature. For the last ten rounds there was not a chance of success; still his olden skill made him difficult to beat, and Cribb, slow and sure, never threw away a chance. Belcher's knuckles of his right hand were swelled immensely, and his right forearm covered with bruises from stopping Cribb's left hand. At the end of forty minutes, at the urgent request of his backers and friends, Belcher gave in, never again to enter the field of honour.

Jem Belcher returned to The Two Brewers and then moved on to his final pub, The Coach and Horses in Frith Street, Soho. He began to drink and gamble heavily and lost most of the money he'd won as a fighter. On one occasion during this period he was arrested for taking part in a drunken brawl and spent 28 days in prison. On his release he became more and more morose and spent hours sitting all alone in his pub probably contemplating what once he'd been and what now sadly he'd become. His customers started to fall away because he was no longer the jovial host of old. He became very ill and his once magnificent athletic figure shrank to a mere bag of bones and he died, probably of cirrhosis of the liver, on 30 July 1811, aged just 30.

The great Jem Belcher, the 'Napoleon of the Ring', was buried at Marylebone burial ground the Sunday following his death. Huge crowds paid their last respects, convinced they'd seen the passing of the greatest fighter who ever lived. No other boxer had ever displayed the brilliant grace, the precision in attack and science in defence like James Belcher, a true Bristol hero and one of the all-time sporting greats.

Jem Belcher was inducted into the International Hall of Fame in 1992.

HENRY PEARCE
'THE GAME CHICKEN'

THE STORY OF HENRY PEARCE, KNOWN AFFECTIONATELY AS The Game Chicken, is the classic tale of a sporting superstar who has a meteoric rise to fame but then almost instantaneously combusts. Pearce, who was born in Bristol in 1777, got his nickname from the abbreviated version of his first name; he always claimed he was christened 'Hen'. He started boxing for money at a very early age when his father used to take him around the Bristol pubs and challenge anyone of similar age and size to fight him. Legend has it that he was never beaten. Later, he served his apprenticeship as a butcher to a tradesman in the city, fighting for money whenever the opportunity presented itself.

There is no record of his early fights but Pearce must have been a talented boxer for Jem Belcher, his great friend and the former champion, to invite him to London to try his hand against the more experienced pugilists of the day. Rather than put him in the ring immediately Belcher and 'The Fancy', the aristocratic patron/gamblers who controlled the sport, decided to try him out in private first – in a small back room of a sporting club against Jack Firby, 'The Young Ruffian' who'd been a former opponent of Belcher. After ten desperate rounds of fierce fighting which left the white coats of the city swells who were watching splattered with blood, the Chicken emerged victorious.

At this time Joe Berks (see Jem Belcher chapter) was claiming the championship but on hearing of the arrival of a new Bristol star he began boasting of what he would do

Hen (Henry) Pearce: a new Bristol star

to him if ever the two should meet. On 11 August 1803 they were both at Shooter's Hill in London, enjoying a day of bear baiting, cock fighting and boxing. The two rivals eyed each other up and words were exchanged and later that evening they met again, at the Fives Court in Little St Martin's Lane. Pearce, very much against his will, was persuaded by friends not to get involved and reluctantly returned to his lodgings and went to bed. Berks, however, continued with his boasting and told Pearce's friends to 'Bring the turnip-headed countryman here and I'll settle him right off!' As Berks was already on remand for £400 for taking part in another fight this contest if it materialised would have to be held very much in private. The news was communicated to Pearce who immediately rose from his bed and went to Jem Belcher's pub, The Two Brewers in Wardour Street, where he found Berks waiting for him. Berks was much the bigger man and came with a fierce reputation of being wild and unpredictable. Standing 6' 2" and weighing over 14 stone he towered over Pearce who, at 5' 8¾" and 11 stone 7 pounds, was small for a boxer.

As the fight was held in the confined space of a private room it was solely a question of who could hit the hardest and quickest. Little skill and science came into it and after fifteen rounds lasting 20 minutes Pearce's powerful punches knocked Berks out cold. However, Berks wasn't satisfied with the result, claiming he'd had too much to drink that night and so a rematch was arranged for Wimbledon Common, on 23 January 1804 for a purse of £100. Thousands of boxing fans turned up to see what was in effect a fight for the championship. The odds were 7-4 in favour of Pearce.

Jack Firby, 'The Young Ruffian': lost to Belcher and Pearce

ROUND 3. Berks, though bleeding profusely, stood up well to his man, and a good display of hits were made on both sides. Berks again thrown.

ROUND 15. The Chicken so much the favourite, that the odds were four to one upon him. It was manifest that Berks was not a match for his man. His style of fighting was considerably inferior to that of his opponent's and he began to appear much distressed.

ROUND 20. Berks's passion now was exhausting his strength. His nose was bleeding considerably and irritated in mind that no chance was being offered of proving successful, he ran in furiously upon his opponent. His intemperance rendered him a complete object for punishment, and the Chicken milled him in every direction. (Even bets that Berks don't come again.)

ROUND 21. Passion uppermost; Berks desperate in the extreme and by running in headlong missed putting in a hit and fell. Pearce smiling at his want of prudence, and holding up both his hands in triumph.

ROUND 24. Berks still insensible to prudence, and determined to get to his man, received a severe milling. He was several times advised by his backers and seconds to give in, but resolutely refused, however at the close of the round was hit down stupefied, but suddenly recovering, gave in.

Henry Pearce was a modest man and after the fight he didn't stay to receive the congratulations or join the celebrations. He was seen jumping onto the back of a coach to London. His second, Bill Gibbons, went to track him down and made enquiries at every inn along the way. He eventually found him in a public house in Chelsea, cooking chops on the tap room fire. Pearce invited Gibbons to join him which he did, but never once mentioned the fight.

Pearce didn't fight again for another year, being advised by Jem Belcher to keep a low profile as the authorities were trying to clamp down on boxing. They'd recently introduced horse patrols which made staging fights much more difficult. Pearce's next contest was on 11 March 1805 against Elias Spray, a coppersmith from Bristol. The original site chosen was Hampton Court, but this had to be changed at the very last minute to Moulsey Hurst (Molesworth Meadow) just across the river because the magistrates had got wind of the fight. It was obvious from the very beginning that Spray wasn't in the same class as Pearce but nevertheless he was a game opponent.

ROUND 6. Both fought well; some sharp blows exchanged. Spray struck his opponent in the stomach. Pearce rallied, and threw him cleverly.

ROUND 7. Pearce seemed much affected by Spray's last blow in the bread basket. He made a hit, but failed, and fell. (Odds fell to 2-1.)

ROUND 12. Spray put in some good determined blows, but they mostly fell short; at length, by a successful blow on the nose he brought down the Chicken.

ROUND 13. Pearce bled profusely. Spray evinced weakness, made a short blow, and fell.

ROUND 14. Pearce met his antagonist with determined resolution, and put in so severe a blow on the jaw, that everyone feared lest he had broken it; Spray fell. (Odds now rose 10-1 on Pearce.)

ROUND 17. Spray attempted to rally but received a most desperate blow upon the temple that nearly deprived him of his recollection and which spoiled him for the rest of the fight. The ensuing five rounds upon the part of Spray were little better than mere exhibitions of animal courage.

ROUND 28. Spray could scarcely stand, yet could not bring himself to say 'No'. He put up his hands and endeavoured to face his opponent. It was all up; the Chicken hit him as he liked, and finally knocked him off his legs.

Gully against Pearce

The fight ended after 29 rounds and 35 minutes when Spray's men mercifully threw in the sponge. Henry Pearce was now widely recognised as the Champion of England and immediately he accepted an offer to meet Stephen Carte, the Midlands Champion, within the next six weeks. Carte was a giant of a man standing 6' 4" and weighing over 16 stone, and although not possessing the skill and experience of Pearce he'd never been beaten in battle. The pair met on 27 April 1805, at Shepperton Common near Chertsey in Surrey and by all accounts it was a one-sided affair with Carte being hopelessly outclassed. Pearce was renowned for the power of his punches, particularly with his left hand and he pummelled Carte's face and ribs mercilessly until after 25 rounds that had lasted thirty five minutes he landed a terrific punch on the point of Carte's jaw that knocked the Midlander senseless.

The Game Chicken's next fight came about through unusual circumstances. As recounted earlier, his Bristol friend, John Gully, had fallen upon hard times and because of debt had ended up in the King's Bench Prison. Pearce heard about his friend's misfortune and took it upon himself to visit him in prison. This led eventually to 'The Fancy' sponsoring a fight between Gully and Pearce at Hailsham in Sussex, in October 1805.

After more than an hour's ferocious battle, Pearce emerged the battered winner. This momentous meeting is described in some detail in the next chapter. The Gully fight had silenced all those who had doubts about Pearce's claim to be the undisputed champion but a big surprise lay in store for him. His great friend and patron Jem Belcher, the former undefeated champion, had become jealous of all the adulation his fellow Bristolian was receiving and challenged him to a fight for 500 guineas 'play or pay' within two months. Belcher claimed he had never officially retired from the ring and was insulted when Pearce had the audacity to call himself champion. The Chicken had no choice. He either had to resign the championship or fight his former friend and mentor. Reluctantly he chose the latter.

Not even the tragic news of Nelson's death at Trafalgar could curb the public's enthusiasm for the fight and on 6 December 1805, just two days after the body of England's hero arrived back at Portsmouth, the fight took place at Barnby Moor near Doncaster in front of a crowd estimated

The great contest between Spring and Langan at Worcester Race-course on 7 January 1824, for the championship of England

to be upwards of 25,000 people.

When the men appeared in the ring Pearce looked much the stronger of the two but the early stages of the fight were dominated by the former champion. However as the contest went on Pearce's strength and better physical condition began to give him the advantage.

> **ROUND 10**. Somewhat in favour of the Chicken, without any blows of consequence. Belcher appeared to be fast growing weak.
>
> **ROUND 14**. Belcher shy and bleeding in the head and body with blows given in the former round. The Chicken followed him to the ropes, when he gave him a hard blow under the blind eye, through his guard, and threw him easy.
>
> **ROUND 15**. This round left no hopes for Belcher; it also decided many bets respecting the first knock down blow. The Chicken went in very gay, and gave his opponent two hits; they closed, and the Chicken hit Belcher a blow underneath, on the lower rib, which to use the sporting phrase doubled him up together, and he fell. The umpire to the satisfaction of the sporting men, declared this to be a knock down blow.
>
> **ROUND 18**. Belcher could not move his left arm from his side; he, however, stood up to fight the

eighteenth round, but finding himself totally disabled he resigned the contest after fighting 35 minutes. The Chicken immediately leaped over the rope out of the ring, and entered it again in the same manner, displaying his agility by a somersault.

The handicap of being blind in one eye had proved to be too much for Belcher. His blows were off target and he couldn't see the hits coming towards him until it was too late to prevent them landing. Several times during the course of the fight Pearce had Belcher at his mercy but always refrained from landing the critical blow. In the twelfth round when he had Belcher trapped on the ropes he cried out, 'I'll not hit thee Jem, lest I hurt thine other eye!' This was a gesture practically unheard of in the pugilistic era. After it was all over Pearce claimed there were several moments in the fight when he had it in his power to kill his former friend.

Pearce was now at the peak of his powers, undefeated Champion of England, but sadly like so many fighters before him and since he took no heed of the advice of his friends on how to look after himself. He spent too much of his time in the London gin palaces in the company of women from opposite spectrums of society. His health declined rapidly and it didn't come as too much of a surprise to anyone who knew him when he announced his retirement from boxing. He returned to Bristol to become a publican.

We next hear of The Game Chicken in 1807 when a fire broke out at Mrs Denzill's, a silk mercer, in Thomas Street, Bristol. A servant girl was trapped high in an attic and her screams for help were going unanswered until Henry Pearce, who happened to be in the vicinity, stepped forward. Showing no regard for his own personal safety he climbed onto the roof of the building next door and with the flames shooting up all around him and the building in danger of collapse he hauled the girl to safety. Once again Pearce became a hero and in *Arliss's Magazine* and the 'Poets' Corner' of *Felix Farley's Bristol Journal* the following poem was published:

In Bristol city, while a house in flames
Fills the beholders with amazement dire,
A damsel at an upper window claims
Their utmost pity, for the approaching fire –
Which every moment seems to gather near,
Nor hope of rescue does there aught appear.

At length upon the neighbouring house top seen,
A gallant youth now hastens to her aid,
And o'er the fearful parapet does lean,
With spirit dauntless, to assist the maid;
Endowed by heaven with more than common might,
He grasps her arms, and draws her to the height.

Oh, glorious act! Oh, courage well applied!
Oh, strength exerted in its proper cause!
Thy name, O Pearce! Be sounded far and wide,
Live, ever honoured, midst the world's applause;
Be this thy triumph! Know one creature saved,
Is greater glory than a world enslaved.

A short time after this brave deed Henry Pearce came to the rescue of another young woman who was being attacked by

Portrait of Henry Pearce, The Game Chicken by William Hobday, 62 x 49 cm. The artist painted a Bristol background as he was living in Bristol at the time and knew Pearce's sister.

three men on Clifton Downs. Pearce intervened on her behalf and took on all three of them in a fight. After receiving a severe beating from the former champion they all apologised to the woman and went off suitably chastised.

For all the glory and fame he brought upon himself and the city of Bristol, Henry Pearce was not a happy man. His wife by all accounts was a shameless drunk whose infidelities drove him wild and some said drove him further to drink. He left Bristol, never to return, and started touring the country giving exhibitions of boxing. His health and fortune were in rapid decline. He was in the vicinity of Oxford giving lessons when Belcher and Cribb had their second fight and after Cribb's victory Pearce informed the champion he hoped he'd soon get well enough to fight him for the title. It was not to be. On the journey across from Oxford Pearce had picked up a cold, which aggravated the pulmonary consumption (TB) he was already suffering from. He was in the last stages of that crippling disease when he took a benefit at the Fives Court on 9 February 1809. His friends were shocked at his appearance. He was too ill to spar and could hardly walk. It was as much as he could do to thank them all for their support. He knew he was dying and he faced death with a calmness and resignation that was typical of the man.

The Game Chicken died on 30 April 1809 at the age of 32, at the Coach and Horses pub in St Martin's Lane, just around the corner from the Fives Court. He was buried at the St James's Church burial ground in St Pancras.

Henry Pearce was a modest man, one of the most heroic and humane champions of England. Although he became champion at a time when there were so many great fighters around he never once allowed his brilliant successes to go his head. He was always the same simple-hearted, honest fellow, kind and generous to a fault who won the affection of everyone he came into contact with. He went down in boxing history as one of England's truly great champions and one of the few who remained unbeaten.

Henry Pearce was inducted into The Ring Boxing Hall of Fame in 1987 and the International Boxing Hall of Fame in 1993.

JOHN GULLY

JOHN GULLY WAS BORN IN WICK NEAR BRISTOL ON 21 August 1783, the son of the publican who kept the Crown Inn in the village. Gully's story is an extraordinary tale of a man who became in turn butcher, prisoner, champion boxer, publican, bookmaker, race-horse owner and breeder, Member of Parliament and finally colliery owner. No other boxer in the history of the sport has had such an amazingly varied career.

Gully's father left The Crown Inn and moved to Bristol to become a butcher and here the youngster learned the trade, in the process developing a strong and powerful physique. Like other young Bristolians of that era Gully was keen to develop his skills with his fists and it wasn't long before he began to earn the respect of his contemporaries in the noble art. His first recorded action as a lad was the thrashing of a local bully who was unfairly setting his dog at a bull he was baiting. To his great surprise Gully learned afterwards his defeated opponent was a prize fighter and the terror of the neighbourhood.

Gully's father died when John was just thirteen and he had to support his widowed mother in keeping the butcher's business going. The family were forced to move to Bath where John had his first recorded fight against a man called Jack Rand at the Lansdown Fair in 1803. There is a story, almost certainly apocryphal, that this Jack Rand was none other than the man who later became known as 'Sixteen String Jack', the notorious highwayman. Gully won

John Gully, born at Wick near Bristol

the fight but the debts incurred in the family business forced him to seek his fortune elsewhere and at the age of 22 he moved to London in an attempt to escape his creditors. They managed to track him down, but to avoid being

The Crown (now the Rose and Crown) at Wick, where John Gully was born in 1783

taken back to Bristol and tried for a more serious offence Gully got himself arrested for a small debt incurred whilst living in London and was duly sent to the notorious King's Bench Prison.

Good fortune was always going to play a major role in Gully's life and here in prison was a classic example. Henry Pearce, the Game Chicken, the champion of England and a good friend of his from his Bristol days, had heard of Gully's misfortune and decided to pay him a visit. The two men indulged in a spot of friendly sparring and Gully put up such an impressive performance that Pearce contacted his backers, Mr Fletcher Reid and Captain Barclay. When these two influential members of 'The Fancy' saw for themselves just how good Gully was they immediately paid off all his debts and obtained his release from prison.

To the surprise of many followers of the 'Ring', including both fighters, Gully was then matched against Pearce for his first major contest. This seemed a little unusual and the rumour spread that the fight was fixed. It didn't add up: two friends from Bristol, the King's Bench Prison story, the same high-profile financial backers all pointed towards something underhand going on even though there was no evidence. Inevitably the police got wind of the fight and marshals were sent out with warrants for the arrest of both fighters. The venue was changed to avoid detection but ultimately amid all the confusion the fight had to be postponed. There were angry scenes and all bets were declared null and void which further fuelled the rumours.

Both Pearce and Gully were very proud men and were dismayed that their honour had been called into question but there was very little they could do to refute the allegations. That surely would have been the end of the matter had not a fortunate incident taken place that again involved John Gully. As was the usual practice of the day professional boxers would tour the country giving exhibitions as a way of supplementing their income. These friendly bouts against local champions with both boxers wearing mufflers or gloves would usually take place in private houses, sporting clubs or pubs.

On one such occasion Gully was sparring with a Corporal of the Guard in a London pub. His opponent was the Army champion standing 6' 3" and weighing nearly 16 stone and a bit of a loudmouth and bully. Even though Gully was giving him a good lesson in the noble art, the Corporal unwisely made the comment that if there was money at stake and the fight was with the 'raw uns' maybe Gully wouldn't put up quite such a good show – an obvious reference to the postponed Pearce fiasco. Gully was incensed, and claimed the army man wasn't fit to wear the King's uniform. Threats were made, a ring was formed and the two men battled it out with bare fists. Gully's honour was at stake and he tore into his opponent with such ferocity that in a very short space of time the army man was left battered and blinded and had to be carried back to his barracks.

The news spread like wildfire amongst the boxing cognoscenti. John Gully was not the push-over they'd been led to believe but a fighter to be reckoned with and the fight with the Game Chicken was re-arranged. It took place on 8 October 1805 at Hailsham in Sussex, and many thousands turned out to see it including the Duke of Clarence, later William IV, and Lord Byron who were both great fans of boxing.

It was by common consent one of the most brutal and bloody fights ever witnessed with the appearance of both fighters at the end of the contest described as truly sickening as the following extract from a contemporary report relates. And remember they were friends!

> **ROUND 4**. Pearce stood up with a smile of confidence on his brow. Both combatants struck at once and both hits were well stopped but Gully fell.
> **ROUND 6**. Pearce put in two good hits right and left and brought Gully down once more. (Odds now rose to 10-2 on the Chicken.)
> **ROUND 12**. Gully threw in a most severe blow, struck Pearce on the mouth and brought him down. Cheers for Gully.
> **ROUND 17**. The best round during the battle, if not that ever was contested. Pearce seemed confident of beating his man and stood up well. Gully rallied, and put in several good blows which were returned by the Chicken without any stopping. Gully brought down his opponent after having successfully planted two good hits on his left eye. This round greatly in Gully's favour and the odds fell, bets being now six to four on the Chicken.
> **ROUND 20**. Pearce seemed almost blind with his left eye, and as blood issued freely, he fought very shy and retreated. Gully followed him up round the ring, and by a good hit brought Pearce down.
> **ROUND 31**. Long sparring. Pearce struck but fell short; Gully was struck over his guard and was thought almost blinded in his right eye.
> **ROUND 33**. Pearce very shy. Gully followed him round the ring but Pearce knocked him down with a blow to the throat.
> **ROUNDS 37-43**. In all these rounds the Chicken had the advantage; both were bleeding freely, particularly Gully, whose ear flowed copiously. Gully appeared shy of advancing; his head dreadfully swollen and

The King's Bench Prison, London, where Gully served time for a bad debt his eyes appeared nearly closed.

The fight followed the same pattern for another 23 gory rounds until finally after much pleading from his seconds and 1 hour, 17 minutes of fighting Gully declined to come up to scratch and Pearce was declared the winner. Both combatants were dreadfully battered and hardly able to see out of either eye. Afterwards both men were acclaimed for their tremendous heroism and bravery. Pearce later acknowledged that Gully was the hardest man he ever fought and the only one that ever stood up to him for so long. 'He has a head for fighting', said the Chicken. 'He must be a sharp chap and get up early as beats John Gully, I can tell thee.'

Two years were to elapse before Gully fought again during which time Pearce had successfully defended his title against the great Jem Belcher and then been forced to retire because of ill health. Although John Gully didn't claim the title himself 'The Fancy', because of his performance against the Chicken, looked upon him as Pearce's natural successor and no one stepped forward to dispute that claim until Bob Gregson the 'Lancashire Giant' issued a challenge. He'd been unbeaten in seven years as a fighter and relied upon his size – he was 6' 2" and weighed over 16 stone – to batter his opponents into submission. The two men met on 14 October 1807 in a valley called Six Mile Bottom on the Newmarket Road and even though Gully, at just 6' and 14 stone, was much the smaller man he started as the 6-4 favourite. It was another titanic struggle, one which for its brutality, heroism and bloodiness would surpass even that of Gully's fight with Pearce.

The contest ended with both men suffering from complete exhaustion and bleeding most severely. Right up to the last it was anyone's fight until finally, in the thirty-sixth round, Gully put in a blow which ended it and Gregson lay for some minutes incapable of moving or speaking.

Amazingly both men appeared on the Newmarket racecourse the following day but Gregson had to be taken home later and seen by a doctor. Most people thought that after taking such a beating Gregson would have had enough but only four weeks after the fight he wrote to Gully. The correspondence gives some indication of how matters were dealt with in those days.

> Mr Gully, It is the wish of myself and friends that I should try my fortune with you in another battle, for £200 a-side. If you are inclined to give me the opportunity, I will thank you to say so, and also to name the time when it will be convenient to meet, to put down stakes and arrange particulars.

Gully was swift to reply:

> Mr Gregson, I will accept your challenge, but wish you would make the match for £250 instead of £200 a-side. I shall not delay a moment in returning to town to make the necessary arrangements as to time, place, etc.

As soon as Gully returned to London the two boxers met, along with their respective backers, and the following contract was drawn up:

> Major Morgan, on the part of Gregson, and Mr.

Jackson, on the part of Gully, agree to deposit 50 guineas each this day, and a further 50 guineas on the 1 March 1808, or forfeit the first 50 guineas; and on the Monday following the Craven meeting, the remainder of the stakes to be made good by the contracting parties, or the 100 guineas to be also forfeited; and that the Hon. Berkeley Craven be requested to hold the stakes on the day of the battle.

CONDITIONS OF THE BATTLE

1st. The battle to take place on the Tuesday following the first spring Meeting, between the hours of ten and twelve, am.

2nd. To fight in a roped square of forty feet.

3rd. Neither to fall without a knockdown blow, subject to the decision of the umpires.

4th. Three umpires to be chosen upon the ground, viz., two, and one in reference.

Signed CHARLES MORGAN
JOHN JACKSON

Bob Gregson: unbeaten in seven years

The return bout generated tremendous interest. It took place at Woburn on 10 May 1808 and people flocked in their thousands to the town to see the big fight for the championship. All available accommodation in all the hamlets and villages around Woburn had been booked well in advance and there wasn't a bed to be had. Men were sleeping fifteen to a room and paying a guinea for the privilege! There was total confusion as the exact spot where the fight was to be staged had to be kept a secret.

The authorities had got wind of the conflict and the Marquis of Buckingham, one of the few aristocrats in those days who was opposed to the sport, assembled a large band of constables and volunteers to try and prevent it taking place. The original venue at Ashley Common was changed at the very last minute and the crowd redirected to Sir John Sebright's private park seventeen miles away. Gully arrived in Lord Barrymore's barouche escorted by about 150 noblemen and gentlemen on horseback and an assortment of gigs and tandems and every other species of vehicle available in those days. Hundreds of other fans from all walks of life arrived on foot or were charged a shilling a mile for the pleasure of riding in the back of a brick cart. It started pouring with rain and at one stage it looked as if the fight would have to be postponed.

After some delay the contest did go ahead and after Tom Cribb's winning battle against Horton it was the turn of Gully and Gregson to enter the ring. Both men fought in white breeches and silk stockings without shoes and just as with the previous set-to it was brutal and unrelenting from the very start.

> ROUND 1. The combatants both sparred about a minute; the utmost silence prevailing in every part of the ring, and everyone had their eyes fixed on the contending champions. Here Gully displayed one of the most signal specimens of boxing that perhaps was ever witnessed, by putting in two most dexterous hits through his opponent's guard, at the same moment in the mouth and throat. Gregson fell like a log and was instantly covered with blood. The greatest commotion now excited, and peal exceeded peal of applause. (The odds rose 6 to 4 on Gully.)
> ROUND 6. Some good rallying but in favour of Gully. Gregson proved incapable of stopping and Gully hit him as he pleased. At the end of the round Gregson put in a tremendous blow on the side of his adversary's head and both fell out of the ring.
> ROUND 7. Gully rallied; put in six successive hits on the side on Gregson's head, and at length knocked him off his legs without the latter getting in one blow.
> ROUND 8. In this round Gregson slightly had the advantage. They closed and Gully received a heavy fall; Gregson's left eye was now almost closed, his nose broken, the blood flowed copiously, and his head was most hideously disfigured.
> ROUND 17. In this round Gregson became intemperate and ran upon his adversary who continued hitting and avoiding him in most surprising manner. Gregson twice turned his back upon his opponent and made towards the ropes, but Gully followed him, changed his front, fibbed him, and kept him from falling, until he had hit him into an almost senseless state, and then dropped him quietly between his arms.

After 28 rounds and one hour and a quarter of bloody fighting Gully emerged victorious but then – at the very height of all the excitement and to everyone's complete surprise, including his backers Captain Barclay and Mr Fletcher Reid – Gully announced his retirement from the ring. He leaned over the ropes of the ring and informed the crowd gathered at the ringside that he wanted to concentrate on being 'mine host' at the Plough Inn in Carey Street, London and would welcome all their custom.

Despite being constantly harassed to change his mind and come out of retirement for 'just one more fight' John Gully kept his word and never fought again but what happened next in his life was truly extraordinary. As the popular landlord of the Plough he developed an interest in horse racing and began to gamble and take bets from his customers. Although sometimes losing very heavily Gully amassed a sizeable fortune and was soon able to purchase Ware Park, a country estate in Hertfordshire. Here he became a successful horse breeder, race-horse owner and a respected member of Tattersall's, the famous London bloodstock auctioneers. In 1832 his horses won the Derby and St Leger and in 1844 he won the Two Thousand

Gully against Gregson. © *Getty Images*

Guineas. In 1846 he won the Derby and Oaks and in 1854 his horses again won the Derby and Two Thousand Guineas. He wasn't always successful, however, and once lost £40,000 by backing one of his horses, Marmeluke, to win the St Leger. Nevertheless he became a very rich man who mixed in society's highest circles and it came as no surprise when in 1832 he turned his attention towards politics. He was elected MP for Pontefract and served two terms until 1837. John Gully features in a famous painting of the House of Commons in 1833 by Sir George Hayter that commemorates the passing of the Great Reform Act of 1832.

After winning the Derby with Andover in 1854 Gully sold off his stud, severed all his racing connections and moved to Marwell Hall near Winchester. His next successful venture came in 1862 when he purchased the Wingate Grange estate and collieries in County Durham. He died on 9 March 1863 at the age of 79, having married twice and fathered 24 children, 12 by each wife. He was buried at the family plot at High Ackworth near Pontefract. Remarkably, he had outlived most of his children one of whom was killed in the Indian Mutiny. Another family member from Bath, also called John Gully, emigrated to New Zealand in 1852 and became one of that country's

John Gully in 1860

most renowned artists.

John Gully brought great honour and glory to the City of Bristol and although he had only two championship fights – both against the same man – his place in boxing history is assured. In his day he was a legend, a true national hero, a man who had literally fought his way out of a debtor's prison to become a Member of Parliament. As a pugilist he will be remembered as a tough, strong, fast,

The private graveyard at St Cuthbert's Churchyard, High Ackworth, the resting place of John Gully and his family

incredibly brave and skilful fighter who, because his career was only brief, probably never reached his full potential. Gully's character is best summed up by Lord William Lennox in his book *Celebrities I Have Known* when he wrote:

> His unpresuming deportment, his great common sense, and the absence of false shame when any reference was made to his early career, fairly earned him that respect which I, and I believe many others retained for him. The memory of John Gully will be cherished by all Englishmen who can appreciate manly courage. His life may point a moral as the special type of one –
> Who through the moil and dust of life
> Went forward undefiled!

John Gully was inducted into The Ring Boxing Hall of Fame in 1959.

TOM CRIBB
'THE BLACK DIAMOND'

So we come to the last and possibly the most famous of the Bristol bare-knuckle champions. Tom Cribb was born in Hanham on 8 July 1781 the son of a coal-working family. He started carrying sacks of coal at a very early age and this enabled him to build up the remarkable strength that was to serve him so well in his later years as a boxer.

At the age of 13 he went to live in London to follow the trade of a bell hanger under the guidance of a relative. The cramped confines of the workplace obviously didn't suit a growing lad so he changed occupations and became first a bargeman on the Thames and then a porter at the wharfs. Both were extremely dangerous jobs and on two occasions he nearly lost his life: once when he slipped and fell between two barges and was nearly crushed to death and again when he slipped and the 500lb load he was carrying fell on his chest and left him coughing up blood for days afterwards. We know that Tom Cribb then joined the Navy and played his part in the Napoleonic War; having done his duty he returned to his previous job on the wharfs as a coal porter and began life as a professional prize fighter.

His first recorded fight, on 7 January 1805, was against George Maddox, one of the most experienced tacticians of the day. The contest took place at Wood Green, near Highgate and Cribb, a mere novice and known in Wapping where he worked as 'The Black Diamond', because of his trade as a coal porter, surprised a great many people when after 67 rounds that lasted two hours twelve minutes he emerged victorious. Three days later he was at The Fives

Thomas Cribb: the greatest of them all

George Nichols: the only man to beat Tom Cribb

Court in London, the favourite meeting place of 'The Fancy' when he was personally challenged by Tom Blake (Tom Tough) to fight within a month for 40 guineas. Cribb had no hesitation in accepting the challenge and the two men met at Blackheath on 15 February when after another hard battle that lasted one and a half hours Cribb was again declared the winner.

This fight seemed to establish Cribb's reputation with 'The Fancy' and some now expressed a desire to back him against any boxer in the country. No one took up their challenge which was hardly surprising for although Cribb wasn't the quickest boxer around at that time he had wonderful defensive qualities, great stamina, a sure punch and was brave beyond belief.

His next encounter – on 21 May 1805 – against a man called Ikey Pig lasted only 11 rounds with Cribb once again emerging victorious. The Black Diamond's star was now in the ascendancy and his backers were rushing him into fights before he'd fully recovered from previous engagements. On 20 July 1805 he suffered his one and only defeat at the hands of the seriously underrated George Nichols from Bristol who it was claimed had won 49 of his previous 50 contests. At least two of these victories were on Durdham Downs, Bristol, one against a man called Hocky Harding for a purse of only a guinea and the other against Harding's brother for a guinea and a half. A third fight for a guinea-a-side was against a sailor weighing 13 stone; it took place in the Back Fields near Lawford's Gate and resulted in yet another win. After he'd defeated all local opposition Nichols's backers decided to move him up in class and a fight with Tom Cribb for a purse of £25 was arranged. It took place at Blackwater, 32 miles from London and Cribb, not surprisingly, started as the odds-on favourite.

ROUND 1. Nichols fights with caution when to the surprise of many he brings Cribb down.
ROUND 4. Cribb puts in a most severe blow and cuts his opponent under the right eye. Nichols still fights with great spirit and perfectly cool and good tempered.
ROUND 20. Nichols perfectly closed one of his antagonist's eyes, notwithstanding he fought with great dexterity, and made several good rallies.
ROUND 40. Cribb appeared distressed in his wind; he, however, had somewhat recovered the sight of his eye, but began to fight very shyly and shift: his

> blows were frequently short and he several times fell back from his own hits.

Cribb had seriously underestimated his opponent and hadn't trained properly for the fight. He had no answer to the defensive tactics adopted by Nichols and after 52 hard rounds lasting an hour and a half he was forced to surrender. It was a shock result and Nichols had the boxing world at his feet but then to everyone's amazement he announced his retirement from the ring and opened up a butcher's shop on Gloucester Lane in Bristol. George Nichols was described by his contemporaries as a quiet, shy, church-going man who had he continued with his boxing career could perhaps have ended up as the greatest of all the Bristol Champions. Sadly we'll never know.

Cribb's comeback fight, for 25 guineas, was on 8 October 1805 at Hailsham, Sussex, on the undercard of the Gully-Pearce battle, and was against Bill Richmond – one of the few black boxers around at that time. After a one-sided fight that didn't attract much attention, Cribb got back to winning ways and came away with the prize money. An interesting side note is that one of the people who saw the fight was the Duke of Clarence.

By now Cribb was considered to be amongst the top-ranked fighters in the country. He now met Captain Barclay of Ury House, Stonehaven in Scotland, a man well-known for his sporting achievements and his methods of getting fit (see Barclay chapter). Barclay once made a bet for a thousand guineas that he could walk a thousand miles in a thousand successive hours. Barclay won the bet and made a fortune. He became a leading figure in bare-fist boxing both as a patron and a trainer. He liked what he saw in Cribb and reckoned he had what it took to become a champion and backed him for 200 guineas against the former champion Jem Belcher. Even though he'd been beaten by the 'Game Chicken' and only had one eye Belcher was still considered a dangerous opponent and thought by many to have too much speed and skill for Cribb to handle.

One of the conditions demanded by Captain Barclay was that Cribb had to follow the strict training schedule he'd prepared for him. This began with his strolling around a country estate for the first two weeks of the programme with gun in hand to 'get the gross humours out of his body'. After this 'The Black Diamond' had to do some serious walking which gradually built up to a punishing programme of walking ten to twelve miles every day, increasing in small stages to 20 miles a day. This included a quarter-mile run at top speed before each walk and another at the end of each day. His food was the simplest: plain joints or steaks underdone and half a pint of old ale twice a day. Under this strict regime Cribb's body weight fell from 15½ stone to just under 12 and Captain Barclay declared him ready.

The fight with Belcher drew a huge crowd and took place on 8 April 1807 at Moulsey Hurst a place that later became known in boxing circles as 'The Cockpit of the Ring'. To give some idea of the popularity of the sport during this period and the kind of distinguished spectator it attracted it's worth mentioning that amongst the crowd who witnessed the fight were the Duke of Clarence, later King William IV, the Duke of Beaufort, the Marquis of Tweeddale, Sir John Lade, Sir John Shelley, and Lord Byron; all happy to ignore the fact that bare-fist boxing was illegal.

Although Belcher started as the 6-4 favourite onlookers

were astonished at the vast improvement shown in Cribb's technique at the beginning of the contest. He looked nothing like the slow, ponderous novice he appeared in previous fights. A contemporary account reads:

> **ROUND 10.** Belcher commenced this round with great spirit and gave Cribb some severe blows, without him having a chance; following and rallying his opponent to the ropes, when Cribb appearing quite fatigued fell. (Odds now rose to four to one on Jem.)
> **ROUND 12.** A small change now making its appearance between the combatants – Cribb seemed rather gaining his strength, while Belcher appeared rather distressed from his exertions; Cribb rallied successfully, planted a hit under Belcher's perfect eye, closed and threw him.
> **ROUND 18.** Belcher put in some severe blows to the body, and followed them with a heavy right-hander to the throat of his opponent, and Cribb fell violently, and quite exhausted. It was in this round that Belcher sprained (broke?) his wrist, and was deprived of the use of his right hand afterwards.
> **ROUND 37.** Belcher had scarcely any strength left to stand, and his brave opponent was not in a much better state, and from this period to the fortieth it was little better than mere hugging. Blows they could not be called, from the exhausted state of both the combatants.

It was still anybody's fight with both fighters at various times appearing to be on top and looking as if they could win. It finally came to an end after thirty five minutes and

'A Striking View' of Bill Richmond.
It can be seen in Bristol City Museum and Art Gallery

in the forty-first round when Cribb put in two violent shoves and Belcher fell exhausted upon the ropes and gave up the contest. It says much for Belcher's skill as a fighter that he was able to last so long against a man who was so much bigger, stronger and fitter than him.

Cribb's next fight was against George Horton, yet another fighter from the Bristol school and a man who had already beaten Tom's younger brother George. This fight took place at Woburn on 10 May 1808 on the under-card of the Gully-Gregson battle and amongst those in attendance were the Duke of Sussex, son of George III and once again Lord Byron. Byron was a huge fan of Cribb's and wrote in his journal after the event that he'd stayed at the same inn as Cribb before the fight and could remember the fighter remonstrating with a waiter 'against the abomination of his towels, which had been laid in lavender!' The fight itself lasted 25 rounds and Cribb restored the family honour by giving Horton a severe beating although as Cribb told Byron afterwards 'He disliked hurting him, he looked so pretty'.

John Gully had retired from boxing after defeating Gregson so the title was now vacant. The sporting world was divided over the merits of Gregson and Cribb as to who would be the next champion so the two were matched to decide the matter at Moulsey Hurst on 25 October 1808. It was an extremely brutal and bloody affair, until finally, in round 23, Gregson failed to come up to scratch. Cribb collapsed exhausted into his second's arms and stayed like that for several minutes before he was able to recover. He was now the undisputed champion of England and was awarded £150 by Captain Barclay for his display of remarkable courage.

To most people's amazement the next man to step forward to challenge Cribb for the championship was none other than Jem Belcher. He was convinced he'd been cheated of victory in their first encounter and the only reason why he eventually lost was because he'd badly damaged his wrist in the eighteenth round. Cribb was more than ready to accept the challenge and their second fight took place on Epsom racecourse on 1 February 1809 for a purse of 200 guineas. Once again Captain Barclay came forward as Cribb's trainer and backer and at the start of the fight the odds were seven-to-four in favour of the champion. During the course of the battle Belcher showed occasional glimpses of his former skills but once again the handicap of having only one eye meant his punches often fell short and Cribb's superior strength and stamina won out in the end. The final rounds were pitiful to watch. The once-great champion was reduced to a mere shell of his former glorious self and his seconds and backers pleaded with him to quit. His strength had gone and his hands were grotesquely swollen. After 31 rounds that lasted 40 minutes Belcher eventually gave in. He never fought again.

Tom Cribb was now at the pinnacle of his career having defeated everyone of note in England, but his next two fights were the ones which were to establish his name forever in the history of British boxing and make him the most famous man in the country. Tom Molineaux, an African-American, had arrived in England unheralded and unknown after having made his way from Virginia where he'd won his freedom from slavery by winning a fight for the plantation owner's son. Molineaux then travelled to New York and earned quite a reputation as a fighter which culminated in his claiming the Championship of America in 1809.

Tom Molineaux was no shrinking violet and on his arrival in London he immediately made for Bill Richmond's pub The Horse and Dolphin in Leicester Square and let it be known he wanted to fight Cribb for the Championship. Richmond himself was a former opponent of Cribb and would have liked nothing better than to get one over on the champion, particularly with the help of another African-American like himself. He arranged for Molineaux to have

Tom Molineaux: his fighting prowess earned his release from slavery

two trial fights in order to gauge his ability and after he destroyed both opponents, one of whom was a Bristol novice named Burrows, Richmond had no hesitation in sending out a challenge to Cribb.

Cribb wasn't keen to fight. He'd recently got married and invested his money in a coal-merchant business and was looking for an easier life but when Molineaux started boasting about what he would do to 'Massa Cribb' when the two of them met he became annoyed and agreed to fight. Cribb hadn't fought for two years but because he hadn't officially retired he was still considered the undisputed champion as no one had stepped forward to challenge him. All that had now changed and the fight with Molineaux was arranged to take place at Copthall Common, near East Grinstead in Sussex, on 18 December 1810 for a purse of 200 guineas a-side.

The forthcoming battle aroused tremendous interest throughout the land. It was the major topic of conversation of the day, not only amongst the fans of boxing but amongst society in general and the issue of course was race. People were alarmed by the fact that a black man, a foreigner, might take the championship away from these shores and Cribb on his part swore that for the honour of old England he'd defend the title with his life. This time, however, he didn't have Captain Barclay's expertise to help him prepare for the fight. Barclay was abroad as part of an expeditionary force fighting the French.

It was a cold, wet and windy day but that didn't stop over 5000 people making their way to Copthall Common, most wading up to their knees in mud along roads and lanes which were virtually impassable. Anyone who was anyone in high society had made it their mission to be there. Cribb at 5' 10½" tall weighed in at 14 stone 3lb whilst Molineaux, at 5' 8¼" and just 1lb lighter, looked the more powerful fighter. The contest itself was a brutal and bloody affair and one of the most controversial fights ever held in England. At the start Molineaux looked confident and was very aggressive and Cribb was taken aback by the strength and agility of his opponent.

Cribb versus Molineaux at Copthall Common, near East Grinstead on 18 December 1810

By the twenty-second round Molineaux had gained the upper hand and the odds had shifted four to one on in his favour. There was an uneasiness about the crowd that they were about to witness the defeat of their champion by a black man from America and Molineaux was subjected to the most appalling racial abuse. Round after round he struck Cribb to his knees and it seemed Cribb was beaten but the crowd kept urging their champion on. In the twenty-eighth round Molineaux won the fight fair and square when Cribb failed to come up to scratch. Three times he was called and three times he failed to make it. Molineaux waited in the centre of the ring ready to be acclaimed the victor but an argument erupted in his corner with one of Cribb's seconds accusing Molineaux of having bullets concealed in his fists. This of course was just a ruse to buy precious time for the champion and by the time

Molineaux had proved his innocence Cribb had recovered sufficiently to continue with the fight.

The disappointment of not winning what was rightfully his together with the cold and wet windy conditions finally began to take its toll on the American.

> **ROUND 23**. In this round Cribb perceiving Molineaux falling off, made play and brought him down, the first time for several rounds.
> **ROUND 29**. Molineaux ineffectually endeavoured to get Cribb's head under his left arm, and also to throw him, but failed in both. The men rallied, and Cribb, who now appeared to possess more confidence than he had for some rounds, knocked his opponent down.

In the next round Molineaux threw Cribb heavily onto the ground and in doing so fell over and hit his head against one of the stakes supporting the ring. Molineaux was dazed and he could hardly lift his arms when Cribb struck him in the throat and down he went again. Molineaux feebly lifted his hand and said to his second 'Massa Richmond, me can fight no more.'

So ended the first World Boxing Championship title fight with a result no Englishman can be proud of. Cribb of course was the hero of the hour and as the winner he'd earned nearly £1000 in stark contrast to Molineaux who, for all his bravery, received a paltry £100. Six weeks later Cribb added considerably to his winnings when a profitable benefit was held in his honour at the Fives Court in London. In the meantime Molineaux had put in for a rematch, claiming the rain and cold had affected his performance and hoping that being 'of a different colour to that of the people amongst whom I have sought protection' would not prejudice his chances. Cribb accepted the challenge but not for less than 500 guineas (250 a-side) a sum Molineaux and his backers were unable to meet.

Once again Cribb went into retirement and Molineaux's backers started hawking their man around the country, giving a series of exhibition fights that made them a great deal of money but did little to enhance the financial fortunes of their fighter. Molineaux was kept quiet by being allowed to indulge himself in drink, food and women. He did, however, go back in the ring and after an easy victory over a Lancashire man called Heskin Rimmer issued a challenge to fight any man in England. There was no one brave enough to take up his challenge so once again Tom Cribb, not wanting to see the championship go abroad, had to step back into the ring.

The return fight took place on 28 September 1811 at Thistleton Gap in Wymondham, Leicestershire and was watched by over 20,000 people, one of the greatest crowds ever to witness a prize fight. Sadly Molineaux's physical condition had greatly deteriorated since their first encounter and it looked as if he hadn't trained. He'd put on a lot of weight and there were rumours circulating that for breakfast that very morning Bill Richmond had allowed him to eat a whole boiled chicken and an apple pie washed down with half a gallon of porter: a dark sweet ale brewed from black malt.

Cribb on the other hand, realising he'd grossly underestimated his opponent in their previous battle, was in magnificent shape for this second fight. Captain Barclay was back from the war and had taken charge of his training routine. Because of the celebrity lifestyle he'd been leading

Cribb versus Molineaux, second fight, staged at Thistleton Gap in Wymondham, Leicestershire on 28 September 1811

Cribb's weight had ballooned up to a corpulent, big-bellied 16 stone but Barclay reduced this to 13 stone 5 ounces by the time he stepped into the ring. The betting reflected his superior condition and he started as the 3-1 on favourite. A contemporary report of their second fight reads:

> **ROUND 2.** Cribb showed first blood at the mouth at setting to. A dreadful rally commenced. Cribb put in a good body hit with the right hand which Molineaux returned on the head with the left flush; both combatants now fought at half arm, and exchanged some half dozen hits with great force.
>
> They then closed and after a severe trial of strength Molineaux threw his opponent. (Odds 6-4 on Cribb.)
>
> **ROUND 4.** In the rally Cribb had hit right and left at the body and head, but Molineaux hit at the head only. He was so successful with the left hand that he planted many flush hits. Both Cribb's eyes were now

Tom Molineaux

damaged, his face dreadfully disfigured, and he bled profusely. Molineaux was evidently in great distress, his chest and sides heaving fearfully. Cribb smiled at such a favourable omen and renewed the rally with a heroism perhaps never excelled. At length Cribb fell, evincing great exhaustion.

ROUND 6. Molineaux distressed for wind and exhausted, lunged right and left. Cribb avoided his blows, and then put in a good hit with his right, which Molineaux stopped exceedingly well. Cribb now got in a destructive blow at his 'mark' which doubled up Molineaux; he got away pitifully cut up; he, however, returned to begin a rally seemingly anxious to go in, but still sensible of the ugly consequences. He appeared almost frantic and no dancing master could perform a pirouette more gratifying to Cribb's friends. Cribb followed him round the ring and after some astonishing execution, floored him by a tremendous hit at full arm's length.

ROUND 7. Molineaux seemed lost in rage. He ran in and undoubtedly did some execution; but Cribb put in several straight hits about the throat, stepping back after each. Molineaux bored in till he fell.

ROUND 9. Molineaux was dead beat, and only stood up to encounter Cribb's ponderous blows. He ran in, Cribb met him with his left hand; the blow was tremendous, being doubled in force by the black's impetuous rush, Molinoueax's jaw was fractured, and he fell like a log. He did not come to time within the half minute, but Cribb, wishing to show his superiority, gave away this chance, dancing a hornpipe about the stage, until –

ROUND 10. With great difficulty Molineaux got off his second's knee, only for fresh punishment. His rush was desperate, but equally unsuccessful, and he fell evidently from exhaustion.

The fight had lasted 19 minutes and ended when Molineaux failed to come up to the mark for the eleventh round. To celebrate his victory Cribb danced a Scotch reel around the ring with John Gully the former champion, who'd acted as his second. It later emerged that Cribb had made £400 for winning the fight whilst Captain Barclay had made £10,000!

Once again Tom Cribb became a national hero and on the Sunday after the fight he was paraded through the streets of London in a barouche and four with the horses decorated with blue ribbons which were his fighting colours. He called in on the unfortunate Molineaux at his quarters to shake his hand and wish him all the best. Banquets were held in Cribb's honour at various sporting establishments in the Capital and he was presented with a Silver Champions Cup, valued at 80 guineas, to mark 'his triumph, his pluck and manly prowess.' In another speech that was made in his honour it was said, 'In combat you gave proof that the hand of a foreigner, when lifted against a son of Britannia, must not only be aided by the strength of a lion, but the heart also.'

After this defeat Molineaux continued fighting but he was never the same force again. He toured the country cashing in on his fame by giving exhibitions and having the occasional fight, winning some and losing some. Anyone who fancied themselves as a fighter would throw their hat into the ring but only those who possessed real skill stood any chance of success. Sadly it was Molineaux's love of life that proved to be his downfall. He liked to be seen wearing the colourful extremes of the fashion of the day and constantly over-indulged in food, women and drink and it was these excesses of the flesh which ultimately led to his ending his days in poverty, riddled with disease. He was travelling around Ireland eking out a pathetic existence giving boxing lessons wherever he could when he fell seriously ill. He relied upon two black soldiers serving with the 77th East Middlesex Regiment in Galway to take care of him and give him food and drink. His once wonderfully impressive physique had shrunk to that of a mere skeleton and he died in the Regimental band-room on 4 August 1818, just seven years after his last fight with Cribb. He was buried in a pauper's grave on Ireland's west coast. The precise location is unknown.

Bill Richmond: an early supporter of Tom Molineaux

After retiring from boxing for the final time Tom Cribb went into business as a coal merchant. This proved unsuccessful so he had to follow the well-worn route of former pugilists and become a publican instead. In 1814 he had the honour to be invited by the Prince Regent to celebrate victory in the Napoleonic War by participating in an exhibition of sparring put on for the King of Prussia at the

Tom Cribb's Cup

house of Lord Lowther in Pall Mall.

Tom Cribb never refused a challenge to his right to call himself champion and in 1821, nearly ten years after his last fight with Molineaux, he was challenged by Bill Neate, another Bristol man, to fight for the title at £200 a-side. Even though he was 40 years old, badly out of condition and suffering from gout Cribb accepted, but when it came to signing the articles for the fight and putting up the money Neate was nowhere to be found.

Cribb was always a great favourite of George IV and at his Coronation, on 19 July 1821, he and other fighters were asked to act as pages and guard the entrance to Westminster Hall, for which duty Cribb was presented with a medal. The last pub he owned was the Union Arms in Panton Street in The Haymarket and this became known as 'Tom Cribb's Parlour' where any evening the host could be found with his 'yard of clay' (pipe) and his glass of 'daffy' (gin) surrounded not only by sportsmen but by artists, actors, men of letters and poets one of whom of course was Lord Byron. A pageant named 'Tom Cribb's Parlour' was written about the pub and often performed on the stage of the Adelphi Theatre.

One of many stories about Cribb's exploits relates to the time when he was training for his fight with Gregson and was taking his exercise through a country village accompanied by his good friend John Gully. Both men were dressed in long smock coats so it wasn't really obvious that they were pugilists in training. Suddenly they came across a group of men one of whom, a giant of a man, was cruelly beating a pig with a stick. Cribb inquired of the man if it was his pig and when told it belonged to a neighbour Cribb politely asked him to stop. The man started to hurl abuse at Cribb and relying on his massive size and the help of his pals threatened to give him and Gully a good hiding. The man approached Cribb in menacing fashion with his fists clenched ready for action. He aimed a violent blow at the champion's head which Cribb stopped with the utmost ease and then put in his famous one-two which floored the bully immediately. 'His nob was materially shook and the claret tapped in a masterly style.' Cribb then proceeded to give the man a lecture on cruelty, foul language and bad manners. Meanwhile Gully fancied a bit of the action himself and asked if any of the other men wanted a go at him. Not surprisingly none took him up on his offer. Only when the men returned to their village did they learn that it was Cribb and Gully they'd had their argument with.

Declining health, domestic troubles and money worries reduced Tom Cribb to a mere shadow of the great pugilist he once was and he was finally forced to give up The Union Arms and go and live with his son, a baker, in the High Street, Woolwich. His last public appearance was on 12 November 1840 when he took a benefit at the National Baths, Westminster Road. At his son's house he was often visited by his friends Byron and Gully and former and present champions. On one such occasion he sat up in bed with his eyes alight with excitement and struck out a right and a left showing, 'How battles were won.' 'Ah!' said a visitor, 'You have not forgotten days of yore.' 'No,' said Cribb, 'There's the action but the steam has gone' and he fell back exhausted.

Tom Cribb died, aged 66, on 11 May 1848. At his funeral thousands lined the streets to pay their last respects to a man of indomitable courage, kindness, integrity and fair play. A few years after his burial it was decided to erect a monument over his grave in the Woolwich churchyard. The editor of *Bell's Life*, the leading sports paper of the day, in England, wrote about this event in 1851:

AN ILLUSTRATION OF THE

Coat of Arms,

ENGRAVED UPON THE SILVER CUP

Presented to TOM CRIBB,

Designed and executed at the expressed wish of the

Higher Flights of the Fancy,

AND GIVEN

As a REMEMBRANCER of their approbation of the manly combats and pugilistic qualities of the

CHAMPION of ENGLAND.

THE CREST:

The *Bristol* Arms.

In the first quarter:

The BRITISH LION is looking down with stern regard on the *American* Flag, half-mast high (*in the fourth quarter;*) the Beaver, symbolic of the latter country, hiding his head under its folds, alluding to MOLINEAUX'S DEFEAT.

In the second quarter:

The Combatants are setting-to; and

In the third quarter:

CRIBB is viewed in his coal barge, illustrative of his trade.

THE SUPPORTERS

Represent the CHAMPION looking with an eye of commiseration on his vanquished opponent.

MOTTO:

"And damn'd be him who first cries, Hold! ENOUGH!"

1813.] *Shakspeare.*

Tom Cribb's Cup explained

Cribb and Molineaux square up to each other as Staffordshire figures.
There was a craze at the time to commemorate sporting events in pottery

Tom Cribb in his prime

Cribb's tomb, Woolwich

As a professor of his art he was matchless, and as a demonstrator of fair play, in principle and in practice he was never excelled. He had still a higher virtue, displayed in sustaining throughout his gallant career, independent of indomitable courage – a reputation for unimpeachable integrity and unquestionable humanity. His hand was ever open to the distresses of his fellow creatures, and whether they befell friend or foe, he promptly, by relieving them, exhibited the influence of the charitable and kindly impulses of a truly benevolent heart – an example well worthy of imitation, and justly entitling him to the present distinction, which, whilst it cherishes his memory, will show to others of his class, who follow in his steps, that their good deeds will live beyond the grave.

The monument, depicting a lion grieving over the ashes of a British hero, can still be seen today, a fitting tribute to a brave-hearted gladiator who, if not the most scientific of the champions, was certainly one of the most loved and respected.

Tom Cribb was inducted into The Ring Boxing Hall of Fame in 1954 and the International Boxing Hall of Fame in 1991.

The great fight between Johnny Broome and Jack Hannan for £1000, on 26 January 1841 at New Park Farm near Bicester

CAPTAIN ROBERT BARCLAY

No mention of the life and times of the bare-fist fighters of the early nineteenth century would be complete without an account of the life of Captain Robert Barclay-Allardyce, Laird of Ury, soldier and sportsman extraordinaire.

Barclay was born at Ury House just outside Stonehaven in Scotland on 25 August 1797. At the age of eight he was sent to Richmond School in England to be educated and this was followed by three years at the Brixton Causeway. Later, at Cambridge University, he was one of the early pioneers of university boxing. His father had married Sarah Ann Allardyce, a descendant of Robert II of Scotland, and this prompted Barclay to adopt her surname at the end of his own although he was always known to the sporting crowd as Captain Robert Barclay. The family who founded Barclay's Bank were descendants of his great-grandfather.

Barclay succeeded to his father's estates at the age of 18 and although he took his responsibilities as a land owner very seriously, it was his love of pedestrian exercise and gambling that was to bring him fame and fortune. Barclay was blessed with having been born into a family renowned for their physical prowess. Bull wrestling, carrying sacks of flour with their teeth, hammer throwing and caber tossing came easy to the Barclays. From a very early age Robert was encouraged to produce prodigious feats of strength and endurance and as a young boy he was able to wield a two-handed sword that most men found difficult to lift. In

Captain Barclay: famed for his long-distance walks

April 1806, whilst serving with his regiment in Suffolk, he made a bet for 1000 guineas that he could lift a half-ton weight off the ground. He won the bet.

Remarkable though these feats of strength were, it is for his exploits as a long-distance walker that Barclay is best remembered. He managed to develop a unique style of walking whereby he would lean forward quite distinctively so that his whole weight was on his knees and he'd only raise his feet a few inches off the ground. By adopting this technique he was able to move at a speed of six miles per hour and cover anything between 20 or 30 miles before breakfast on most days of the week.

When participating in his long-distant walks Barclay declined the use of the more acceptable athletic attire of the day, preferring instead to wear a top hat, cravat, warm woollen suit, lamb's wool socks and thick-soled shoes. Proof that this didn't seem to diminish his performance in any way can be seen in the following list of some of his pedestrian achievements.

August 1796. Won a bet for 100 guineas with a gentleman from London to walk six miles within an hour.

1798. He beat Fergusson the celebrated walking clerk in a walking race over 70 miles. It took Barclay 14 hours and he won by several miles.

December 1799. He walked 150 miles in two days, from Fenchurch Street in London to Birmingham via Cambridge.

November 1800. He walked 64 miles in 12 hours (including refreshment) in preparation for a match of 90 miles in 21½ hours for a bet of 500 guineas. Barclay caught a cold and gave up the bet.

1801. Barclay renewed the above bet for 2000 guineas. He accomplished 67 miles in 13 hours when he drank some brandy and was sick. Barclay gave up the bet and the umpires went home.

10 November 1801. He repeated the above bet of walking 90 miles in 21½ hours for 5000 guineas. He won with one hour, seven minutes and 56 seconds to spare.

1802. Walked 64 miles in ten hours.

1806. Walked 100 miles in 19 hours.

October 1808. Made a bet with a Mr Webster to walk a thousand miles in a thousand successive hours at a rate of a mile in every hour for a prize of 1000 guineas.

Between 1 June and 12 July 1809 enormous crowds turned up at Newmarket to see Barclay win the above bet. Not a bed could be found at any of the towns or villages around Newmarket. It was estimated that over £100,000 – an immense amount in today's money – was bet on the result. Barclay himself had many side bets and as a result his final profit on the walk amounted to over £16,000. During the 42 days of the walk his body weight dropped from 13 stone 4lbs, to 11 stone.

Captain Robert Barclay had joined the 23rd Regiment of Foot in 1805 and in 1809, just two days after his epic thousand-mile walk, he served as the aide-de-camp to the Marquis of Huntley on the ill-fated Walcheren Expedition. Walcheren was the fever-ridden island at the mouth of the River Scheldt, a base used by the British Forces before the planned attack on the French-controlled naval base at Antwerp. The British lost 7000 men out of a force of 40,000 with only 106 actually killed in action. Most of the casualties were caused by malarial fever and Barclay himself became very ill. Fortunately he was saved by his strong constitution and returned to Scotland to recuperate, bitterly disappointed at not being able to attend the first Cribb versus Molineaux fight.

Robert Barclay was far from being a modest man and as well as having a gigantic nude statue of himself in Herculean pose placed in the hall of his house at Ury he made several claims through his lawyers to the earldoms of Airth and Menteith, both of which were thrown out by the House of Lords. One claim which he didn't pursue, the earldom of Strathearn, would have led to his being named the rightful King of Scotland! Barclay also harboured ambitions to enter Parliament but was thwarted in his attempts by people in high places who had nothing but contempt for a man involved in illegal prize fighting.

In his fifties Barclay started a new business venture. He launched the 'Defiance' stagecoach which ran between Aberdeen and Glasgow and this soon earned itself the reputation of being the most efficient and reliable stagecoach Scotland had ever seen. The thrill of breaking records never seemed to leave him and he once single-handedly took the London mail coach to Aberdeen staying

Captain Barclay in walking attire

in the driver's seat for three days and nights.

Barclay kept himself fit throughout his life and fathered four children by two different women, neither of whom he married. His last child was born when he was in his seventies. Barclay died of paralysis at his home in Ury, Kincardineshire on 8 May 1854 as a result of injuries he received when he was kicked by a horse. He was 79.

As the trainer and backer of Tom Cribb, Barclay's place in boxing history is assured but it should also be remembered that he was very much the founding father of pedestrianism which developed into what is known today as race-walking. His training methods of diet and exercise were revolutionary in their day and set the standards to follow for years to come.

The Tom Cribb, Panton Street, The Haymarket, London. Formerly The Union Arms and scene of 'Tom Cribb's Parlour', Cribb was landlord here from 1825 to 1834. It was renamed the Tom Cribb in 1960

LIST OF ILLUSTRATIONS

Bibliography

Pierce Egan, *Boxiana*: *Vols 1 and 2*, G Smeaton, London, 1813.

Pierce Egan, *Sketches of Pugilism,* G Smeaton, London, 1818.

Fred Henning, *Fights for the Championship*: Vols 1 and 2, published by *Licenced Victuallers Gazette,* 1903.

Daniel Mendoza, *The Memoirs of the Life of Daniel Mendoza,* London, 1816.

W Oxberry, *Pancretia: A History of Pugilism*, London, 1812.

Bohun Lynch, *The Prize Ring*, Country Life Ltd., London, 1925.

Henry Downes Miles, *Pugilistica: Vols 1 and 2*, John Grant, Edinburgh, 1906.

Acknowledgements

Anton Bantock, local historian

Sheena Stoddard, Bristol City Museum and Art Gallery

Paul Norris, photography

Stuart Hobday

Melissa van Vliet, Christie's

Roger Curtis

INDEX